Mahamudra Tantra

THE SUPREME
HEART JEWEL NECTAR

THARPA PUBLICATIONS
Ulverston, England
Glen Spey, New York

First published 2005.

The right of Geshe Kelsang Gyatso
to be identified as author of this work
has been asserted by him in accordance with
the Copyright, Designs, and Patents Act 1988.

Tharpa Publications
Conishead Priory
Ulverston
Cumbria LA12 9QQ, England

Tharpa Publications
47 Sweeney Road
P.O. Box 430
Glen Spey, NY 12737, USA

© Geshe Kelsang Gyatso and New Kadampa Tradition 2005.

Line illustrations by Gen Kelsang Wangchen.

Library of Congress Control Number: 2005923969

British Library Cataloguing in Publication Data
Kelsang Gyatso, 1931-
Mahamudra Tantra:
an introduction to meditation on Tantra
1. Mahamudra (Tantric rite)
2. Meditation - Tantric Buddhism
1. Title
294.3′4435

ISBN 0948006 93 5 – paperback
ISBN 0948006 94 3 – hardback

Set in Palatino by Tharpa Publications.
Printed on Wentworth Opaque, acid-free 250-year longlife paper and
bound by The Cromwell Press, Trowbridge, Wiltshire, England.

Contents

Illustrations

The line illustrations depict the Mahamudra Lineage Gurus.

Preface

This book, which I have prepared for the people of this modern world, is a practical guide to discovering the real meaning of human life. Generally, according to our common experience, there is no real meaning in this ordinary human life. Many old people or those very close to dying understand how human life is empty and hollow. Throughout our life we try very hard to accumulate so many things such as wealth and possessions, but finally without choice everything that belonged to us passes to others; we can carry nothing with us to our next life. The real meaning of human life is finding and following the correct path to enlightenment, and the supreme correct path to enlightenment is Highest Yoga Tantra, especially Mahamudra Tantra.

If we sincerely wish to practise the instructions on Mahamudra Tantra presented in this book, we should first receive the empowerment of Buddha Heruka and gain complete understanding of the meaning of these instructions. Then, through putting these instructions into practice, we can fulfil our ultimate goal.

Geshe Kelsang Gyatso
January 2005, Happy New Year!

PART ONE

Introduction to Tantra

Buddha Shakyamuni

Basic View

Mahamudra Tantra is a quick method for attaining enlightenment, and the instructions on this practice are very profound. For our practice of Mahamudra to be effective we need a firm foundation in basic correct view and intention. Just as we cannot build a house properly without a basic foundation, we cannot practise Mahamudra effectively without first accomplishing this basis, and without understanding its meaning clearly.

Our normal view is that our daily experiences, whether unpleasant or pleasant, come from external sources. Following this view we dedicate our whole life to improving our external conditions and situation, but still our human problems and suffering increase year by year. This clearly indicates that our normal view is incorrect, and only deceives us. Incorrect views and intentions cause us to follow wrong paths that lead to suffering, whereas correct views and intentions enable us to follow spiritual paths that lead to happiness.

In this context, 'paths' do not mean external paths that lead from one place to another. We do not need to study external paths as we can see them directly with our eyes. 'Paths' here refer to internal paths, which are by nature our actions. Actions of body, speech and mind that are motivated by ignorance are wrong paths because they lead to suffering, and actions that are motivated by wisdom are correct paths – or spiritual paths – because they lead to happiness.

Because there are different levels of happiness, such as the happiness of liberation and enlightenment, there are different levels of spiritual paths, such as the path to liberation and the path to enlightenment. These paths can be further divided into the path of accumulation, the path of preparation, the path of seeing, the path of meditation and the Path of No More Learning. Moreover, because there are different levels of suffering, such as the sufferings of humans, animals and hell beings, there are different levels of wrong paths, such as those that lead to rebirth as a human being, animal or hell being. By studying the different types of paths presented by Buddha we can distinguish between correct and incorrect paths, and thereby avoid incorrect paths. Then, by entering, making progress on and completing correct spiritual paths, we can attain enlightenment and thus accomplish the real purpose of our human life.

In *Guide to the Middle Way* the famous Buddhist scholar Chandrakirti lists seven types of internal path:

1 Actions that lead to the happiness of great enlightenment

2 Actions that lead to liberation
3 Actions that lead to rebirth as a god
4 Actions that lead to rebirth as a human being
5 Actions that lead to rebirth as an animal
6 Actions that lead to rebirth as a hungry spirit
7 Actions that lead to rebirth as a hell being

The first two are supramundane paths, which are correct spiritual paths that lead to great enlightenment and liberation. There are many levels of these paths corresponding to the many levels of spiritual attainment that are explained in teachings on the stages of the path, Lamrim. For example, *The New Meditation Handbook* explains twenty-one different meditations that accomplish twenty-one spiritual paths, or stages of the path to enlightenment. Traditionally, the first of these is strong reliance on our Spiritual Guide. As Je Tsongkhapa says in *Prayer of the Stages of the Path*:

> The path begins with strong reliance
> On my kind Teacher, source of all good.

All these twenty-one stages of the path, beginning with reliance on our Spiritual Guide, are spiritual paths that lead to pure and everlasting happiness.

The remaining five paths listed by Chandrakirti are mundane paths, which are incorrect paths that lead to states of suffering. They are also called 'contaminated actions' because they are motivated or contaminated by the inner poisons of self-cherishing and self-grasping ignorance. Even virtuous actions that are motivated by self-grasping ignorance, and that lead to human rebirth, are contaminated actions. In our previous lives, motivated by the delusion of self-grasping, we performed virtuous actions such as observing moral discipline. This action was the main cause of our present human rebirth, but because it was contaminated by delusions our present human rebirth is a contaminated rebirth. Because we have taken a contaminated rebirth as a human being, we have no choice but to experience the various kinds of human suffering.

Our present experiences of particular suffering and problems have a specific connection with particular actions we performed in the past. This hidden connection is subtle and not easy to understand. We cannot see it with our eyes, but we can understand it through using our wisdom, and especially through relying upon Buddha's teachings.

Why do we suffer and experience so many problems? Suffering and problems are not given to us as a punishment. Whenever we experience difficulties we usually blame others, but in reality it is because we have taken a contaminated human rebirth as a result of contaminated actions that arose from our own self-grasping and self-cherishing. Our human rebirth is the basis of all our human suffering and problems. Animals have to experience various kinds of animal suffering and problems because they have taken a contaminated animal rebirth. This is also true for hell beings, hungry spirits and even the gods of the desire realm; all living beings experience suffering because they have taken a contaminated rebirth. Such rebirths are the nature of suffering, and are the basis of all unhappiness and problems.

If we use our human rebirth for spiritual practice it becomes meaningful, but otherwise its nature is suffering: it is a manifestation of the poisonous mind of self-grasping. If a seed is poisonous, its resultant crop is poisonous. Similarly, because the cause – a contaminated rebirth – is like poison, its effects are inevitably poisonous and painful.

Contaminated rebirth is like a deep and boundless great ocean, and our problems and sufferings are like waves continually arising from it. We have been in this great ocean since beginningless time, taking contaminated rebirths in life after life. If we do not achieve permanent liberation from taking contaminated rebirths in this life, we shall have to remain in the ocean of suffering for countless future lifetimes; this suffering will never end naturally by itself. For as long as we remain in this great ocean, our bodies will be eaten again and again by the sea monsters of the Lord of Death, and we shall constantly have to experience new rebirths. Then, in each new life, we shall have to experience the suffering and problems of that particular life. If we are born human we have no choice but to experience human suffering and problems, and if we are born an animal we have to experience animal suffering and problems. This cycle of contaminated rebirth and suffering, which is called 'samsara', revolves continually, for life after life, endlessly.

Our contaminated rebirth is our own samsara. Although none of us wants to suffer, because we are in samsara suffering arises naturally without choice. It takes great wisdom to recognize our own samsara and to understand that this is our real situation. The understanding and belief that our own samsara – our contaminated rebirth – is the source and basis of all our suffering and problems is the basic correct view that leads us to the attainment of liberation and enlightenment. Developing and maintaining such a non-deceptive view is the basis for effective practice of Mahamudra Tantra, which is the actual method to cut the continuum of contaminated rebirth.

When, through contemplating these instructions, we understand clearly that all our daily problems and suffering come from our own samsara, we shall strongly believe, from the depths of our heart, that it is extremely important to abandon our own contaminated rebirth and attain permanent liberation from suffering. We should exert great effort in maintaining this beneficial view day and night without forgetting it.

While maintaining this view, we should then consider other living beings. Compared with others our own problems and sufferings are insignificant because others are countless while we ourselves are each just one single person. The happiness and freedom of countless living beings are more important than the happiness and freedom of one single person – ourself. It is therefore inappropriate to be concerned only with our own liberation. We should develop instead the superior view that cherishes all living beings and maintain this day and night, never allowing ourself to forget it.

Basic Intention

Wherever we go and whatever we do depends upon our intention. No matter how powerful our body and speech may be, we shall never be able to do anything if we lack the intention to do it. If our intention is incorrect we shall naturally perform incorrect actions, which give rise to unpleasant results, but if our intention is correct the opposite will be true.

Because of our incorrect or selfish intention we perform contaminated actions, which are the main cause of taking contaminated rebirth – our own samsara. Our own samsara, the source of all our suffering and problems, is therefore created by incorrect intention. Our self-cherishing intention wants us to be happy all the time while neglecting others' happiness. This is the normal intention that we have had since beginningless time, day and night – even during sleep – in life after life. However, until now we have never fulfilled this wish. This is because in this cycle of contaminated rebirth there is no real happiness at all.

Bodhisattva Manjushri

In *Prayer of the Stages of the Path* Je Tsongkhapa says:

Samsara's pleasures are deceptive,
Give no contentment, only torment.

Many people think 'If I become rich, have a good position or find an attractive lover, I will be happy', but when they actually become rich, have a good position or find an attractive lover they still do not experience pure happiness. Instead they experience many new problems, sufferings and dangers; we can see many examples of this everywhere!

When we are eating or drinking with our friends or going on holiday, we may feel that we are happy, yet in truth this happiness is not real happiness but only a reduction of our previous problems. The experience of pleasure when eating food, for example, is merely a reduction of hunger, not real happiness. If it was real happiness, then eating food would be a real cause of happiness and it would follow that the more we ate, the happier we would become. But this is impossible! Eating food is actually a real cause of suffering because there comes a point when the more we eat, the more our suffering increases. This deceptive nature can be recognized in all other worldly pleasures.

In *Guide to the Bodhisattva's Way of Life* the great scholar Shantideva says that we need to attain enlightenment because in this samsara there is no happiness. There is no real meaning in this cycle of contaminated rebirth. The only meaning of taking a human rebirth is to attain enlightenment by following the path to enlightenment. This path is very simple. All we need to do is to stop our self-cherishing intention and learn to cherish all living beings equally without discrimination. All other spiritual realizations will naturally follow from this.

Detailed explanations on how to learn to cherish others and how to recognize, reduce and abandon self-cherishing can be found in *Transform Your Life* and *The New Meditation Handbook*. We should continually apply effort in contemplating and meditating on the meaning of these instructions until we gain the deep realization of cherishing all living beings equally. We shall know that we have gained this realization when out of meditation we spontaneously feel that each and every living being, even the tiniest insect, is supremely precious and that their happiness and freedom are most important.

With the realization of cherishing love, we then contemplate how all living beings continuously experience the cycle of contaminated rebirth in life after life – again and again experiencing the sufferings of birth, sickness, ageing, death, having to part with what they like, having to encounter what they do not like, and failing to satisfy their desires. In this way, we shall develop the superior intention that spontaneously wishes to liberate each and every living being from their samsara – the source of all their suffering. This universal compassion and the wisdom of Mahamudra Tantra are like the two wings of a bird: through relying upon them we can fly through the sky of the ultimate truth of all phenomena and quickly reach the supreme ground of enlightenment.

Enlightenment is defined as an omniscient wisdom whose nature is the permanent cessation of mistaken appearance and whose function is to bestow mental peace on all living beings. When we attain enlightenment we become an enlightened being. In Buddhism, enlightened being and Buddha are synonymous. Buddha means 'Awakened One', and refers to anyone who has awakened from the sleep of ignorance and is completely free from dream-like samsaric problems and suffering. The 'sleep of ignorance' is the sleep of self-grasping in which living beings always remain and from which they have never awakened. Through the power of their ignorance, each and every living being without exception experiences mistaken appearance. Because of this they have to experience problems, sufferings, fears and dangers endlessly, throughout their life and in life after life. Only Buddhas are free from this. A detailed explanation of self-grasping ignorance and how to abandon it can be found in Part Three: What is Emptiness?

The nature of a Buddha is complete purity, and the function of a Buddha is to bestow mental peace on all living beings by bestowing blessings. It is for this purpose alone that Buddhas attain enlightenment.

The benefits living beings receive from Buddhas are immeasurable. As it says in *Liberating Prayer*, Buddha is 'the source of happiness and goodness' for all living beings. Through receiving Buddha's blessings each and every living being, even an animal or hell being, occasionally experiences mental peace. At that time, because their minds are peaceful and happy, they are happy. Apart from these occasional moments, their minds are pervaded by the darkness of ignorance and they continually experience various kinds of problems and sufferings in life after life. Buddha's teachings are the only method that can remove the darkness of ignorance from our mind. Through putting them into practice, we can remove the ignorance of self-grasping, and in this way experience permanent liberation from suffering, the permanent inner peace of nirvana.

Buddha's teachings are called 'Dharma'. They are the supreme mirror in which we can see the faults of our delusions and the kindness of all mother living beings, so that we can understand what we need to abandon and what we need to practise. They are the supreme medicine with which we can cure our worst sicknesses of anger, attachment and ignorance, so that eventually we can attain the ultimate goal of human life – enlightenment.

To benefit all living beings, Buddhas emanate as various things, both animate and inanimate. There is no place where there are no emanations of Buddha helping living beings, and there is not one person who is not receiving Buddha's blessings. Even those who deny the existence of Buddha receive Buddha's blessings, and because of this they too occasionally experience mental peace. When their minds are peaceful they are happy, even if their external conditions are poor, but for as long as their minds are unpeaceful they will never be happy, even if they have the very best external conditions. Therefore, the happiness of living beings depends upon their inner peace – their peace of mind – which in turn depends upon receiving Buddha's blessings.

Many times we may try hard to cultivate a peaceful mind, but due to strong delusions we are unsuccessful; yet occasionally we experience inner peace without making any effort from our side. This is because we have received

Buddha's blessings upon our mental continuum. We receive Buddha's blessings only occasionally and not continually because normally our mind is covered by the thick darkness of ignorance.

In his Tantric teachings, Buddha listed many enlightened Deities or Buddhas, such as Heruka and Hevajra. The name Heruka is Sanskrit. 'He' reveals emptiness, 'ru' reveals great bliss and 'ka' reveals the union of great bliss and emptiness. An enlightened being who is imputed upon the union of great bliss and emptiness is real Heruka, definitive Heruka. The body of definitive Heruka is Buddha's Truth Body, or Dharmakaya. It has no colour or shape, and is all-pervasive; there is no place where definitive Heruka is absent. Heruka who appears in the form of a blue-coloured body with four faces and twelve arms embracing Vajravarahi is called 'interpretative Heruka'. When Buddha gave the Heruka empowerment, he appeared in the aspect of interpretative Heruka in order to show the basis, path and results of Highest Yoga Tantra in a manner visible to others.

Buddha's Truth Body, or Dharmakaya, is his omniscient wisdom, which is the union of great bliss and emptiness. Buddha's Truth Body is the basis of imputation of Heruka. According to the appearance of ordinary people Buddha seemed to pass away, but in truth he never passed away because his main body, the Truth Body, is deathless. Understanding the nature and function of Buddha, we should deeply rejoice in his pre-eminent qualities.

As mentioned previously, our universal compassion wishes to liberate all living beings from their suffering. The only method to do this is first to attain Buddhahood ourself because only a Buddha has the power to liberate all living beings from suffering permanently. Contemplating the pre-eminent qualities of Buddha and remembering our universal compassion, we should make a strong determination to attain enlightenment for the benefit of all living beings. We then meditate continually on this determination with single-pointed concentration until we gain the deep realization that spontaneously wishes to attain enlightenment for the benefit of all living beings. This realization is called 'bodhichitta'. We should maintain this compassionate intention day and night, never allowing ourself to forget it.

Developing correct view; learning to cherish others; recognizing, reducing and finally abandoning self-cherishing; and developing universal compassion and the precious mind of bodhichitta, are all included within the common path explained by Buddha in his Sutra teachings. To fulfil quickly the wish of our supreme intention of bodhichitta, Buddha taught the uncommon path of Mahamudra Tantra. This will now be explained.

What is Tantra?

Although Tantra is very popular, not many people understand its real meaning. Some people deny Buddha's Tantric teachings whereas others misuse them for worldly attainments; and many people are confused about the union of Sutra and Tantra practice, mistakenly believing that Sutra and Tantra are contradictory. In *Condensed Heruka Root Tantra* Buddha says:

> You should never abandon Highest Yoga Tantra,
> But realize that it has inconceivable meaning
> And is the very essence of Buddhadharma.

When we understand the real meaning of Tantra there will be no basis for misusing it, and we shall see that there are no contradictions at all between Sutra and Tantra. Practising Sutra teachings is the basic foundation for practising Tantric teachings, and the practice of Tantra is the quick method to fulfil the ultimate goal of Sutra teachings. For example, in his Sutra teachings Buddha encourages us to

Je Tsongkhapa

abandon attachment, and in Tantra he encourages us to transform our attachment into the spiritual path. Some people may think this a contradiction, but it is not, because Buddha's Tantric instructions on how to transform attachment into the spiritual path are the quick method for abandoning attachment! In this way, they are the method to fulfil the aims of Sutra teachings.

As mentioned above, universal compassion accomplished through the practice of Sutra teachings, and the wisdom of Mahamudra Tantra accomplished through the practice of Tantric teachings, are like the two wings of a bird. Just as both wings are equally important for a bird to fly, so both Sutra and Tantra are equally important for practitioners seeking enlightenment.

Tantra is defined as an inner realization that functions to prevent ordinary appearances and conceptions and to accomplish the four complete purities. Although Buddha's Tantric scriptures are sometimes called 'Tantra' because they reveal Tantric practices, actual Tantra is necessarily an inner realization that protects living beings from ordinary appearances and conceptions, which are the root of samsara's sufferings. Tantra, Secret Mantra and Vajrayana are synonymous. The four complete purities are the pure environment, body, enjoyments and activities of a Buddha.

For living beings, the experience of worldly pleasures is the main cause of increasing their attachment, and therefore the main cause of increasing their problems. To stop attachment arising from the experience of worldly pleasures, Buddha taught Tantra as a method to transform worldly pleasures into the path to enlightenment. In accordance

19

with the different levels of transforming worldly pleasures into the path, Buddha taught four levels or classes of Tantra: Action Tantra, Performance Tantra, Yoga Tantra and Highest Yoga Tantra. The first three are called the 'lower Tantras'. In Highest Yoga Tantra, Buddha taught the most profound instructions for transforming sexual bliss into the quick path to enlightenment. Since the effectiveness of this practice depends upon gathering and dissolving the inner winds into the central channel through the power of meditation, these instructions were not explained by Buddha in the lower Tantras. In the lower Tantras, Buddha taught instructions on how to transform worldly pleasures – other than sexual bliss – into the path to enlightenment through imagination, which is a simpler practice of Tantra.

The gateway through which we enter Tantra is receiving a Tantric empowerment. An empowerment bestows upon us special blessings that heal our mental continuum and awaken our Buddha nature. When we receive a Tantric empowerment we are sowing the special seeds of the four bodies of a Buddha upon our mental continuum. These four bodies are the Nature Truth Body, the Wisdom Truth Body, the Enjoyment Body and the Emanation Body. Ordinary beings do not possess more than one body, whereas Buddhas possess four bodies simultaneously. A Buddha's Emanation Body is their gross body, which can be seen by ordinary beings; the Enjoyment Body is their subtle body, which can be seen only by practitioners who have gained higher realizations; and the Nature and Wisdom Truth Bodies are their very subtle bodies that only Buddhas themselves can see.

In Tantra, the principal objects to be abandoned are ordinary conceptions and ordinary appearances. The terms 'ordinary conceptions' and 'ordinary appearances' are best explained by the following example. Suppose there is a Heruka practitioner called John. Normally he sees himself as John, and his environment, enjoyments, body and mind as John's. These appearances are ordinary appearances. The mind that assents to these ordinary appearances by holding them to be true is ordinary conception. The appearances we have of an inherently existent 'I', 'mine' and other phenomena are also ordinary appearances; self-grasping and all other delusions are ordinary conceptions. Ordinary conceptions are obstructions to liberation, and ordinary appearances are obstructions to omniscience. In general, all sentient beings, except Bodhisattvas who have attained the vajra-like concentration of the path of meditation, have ordinary appearances.

Now if John were to meditate on the generation stage of Heruka, strongly regarding himself as Heruka and believing his surroundings, experiences, body and mind to be those of Heruka, at that time he would have the divine pride that prevents ordinary conceptions. If he were also to attain clear appearance of himself as Heruka, with the environment, enjoyments, body and mind of Heruka, at that time he would have the clear appearance that prevents him from perceiving ordinary appearances.

At the beginning, ordinary conceptions are more harmful than ordinary appearances. How this is so is illustrated by the following analogy. Suppose a magician conjures up an illusion of a tiger in front of an audience. The tiger appears

21

to both the audience and the magician, but whereas the audience believe that the tiger actually exists, and consequently become afraid, the magician does not assent to the appearance of the tiger and so remains calm. The problem for the audience is not so much that a tiger appears to them, as their conception that the tiger actually exists. It is this conception rather than the mere appearance of the tiger that causes them to experience fear. If like the magician they had no conception that the tiger existed, then even though they still had an appearance of a tiger they would not be afraid. In the same way, even though things appear to us as ordinary, if we do not conceptually grasp them as ordinary this will not be so harmful. Similarly, it is less damaging to our spiritual development that our Spiritual Guide appears to us as ordinary and yet we hold him or her to be in essence a Buddha, than it is for our Spiritual Guide to appear to us as ordinary and for us to believe that he or she is ordinary. The conviction that our Spiritual Guide is a Buddha, even though he or she may appear to us as an ordinary person, helps our spiritual practice to progress rapidly.

To reduce ordinary appearances and conceptions Buddha taught the Tantra of generation stage; and to abandon these two obstructions completely Buddha taught the Tantra of completion stage, especially Mahamudra Tantra. By completing our training in these Tantras we shall become a Tantric enlightened being, such as Heruka, with the complete purities of environment, body, enjoyments and activities of a Buddha.

The Tantra of Generation Stage

In generation stage, through the power of correct imagination arising from wisdom, Tantric practitioners generate
themselves as Tantric enlightened Deities such as Heruka,
and their environment, body, enjoyments and activities as
those of Heruka. This imagined new world of Heruka is
their object of meditation and they meditate on this new
generation with single-pointed concentration. Through
continually training in this meditation Tantric practitioners
will gain deep realizations of themselves as Heruka, and
their environment, body, enjoyments and activities as those
of Heruka. This inner realization is generation stage Tantra.

Generation stage Tantra is defined as an inner realization
of a creative yoga that is attained through training in the
three bringings. It is called a 'creative yoga' because the
object of meditation is created by imagination and wisdom.
The three bringings are: bringing death into the path of the
Truth Body, bringing the intermediate state into the path of
the Enjoyment Body and bringing rebirth into the path of

Togdän Jampäl Gyatso

the Emanation Body. The main function of generation stage Tantra is to purify ordinary death, intermediate state and rebirth, and to accomplish a Buddha's Truth Body, Enjoyment Body and Emanation Body. Detailed explanations of how to train in the three bringings can be found in other Tantric books such as *Essence of Vajrayana* and *Guide to Dakini Land*.

In generation stage Tantra, practitioners emphasise training in divine pride and training in clear appearance. Before training in divine pride, practitioners need to learn to perceive their body and mind as Heruka's body and mind. Having accomplished this, they then use their imagined Heruka's body and mind as the basis of imputation for their 'I' and develop the thought 'I am Buddha Heruka.' They then meditate on this divine pride with single-pointed concentration. Through training in this meditation they will gain a deep realization of divine pride, which spontaneously believes that they are Heruka. At this time they have changed the basis of imputation for their I.

From beginningless time, in life after life, the basis of imputation for our I has been only a contaminated body and mind. Because our I is imputed upon a contaminated body and mind, whenever we develop the thought 'I' we simultaneously experience the ignorance of self-grasping, a mind grasping at an inherently existent 'I' and 'mine', which is the root of all our sufferings. However, for qualified Tantric practitioners, their deep realization of divine pride prevents the ignorance of self-grasping from arising so there is no basis for their experiencing suffering; they will enjoy their pure environment, body, enjoyments and mind of Heruka.

We may ask how, if these practitioners are not yet actually Buddha Heruka, they can believe that they are; and how is it possible for them to gain the realization of divine pride if their view believing themselves to be Heruka is a mistaken view? Although these practitioners are not real Buddha Heruka, nevertheless they can believe that they are because they have changed their basis of imputation from their contaminated aggregates to the uncontaminated aggregates of Heruka. Believing themselves to be Buddha Heruka is not a mistaken view because it is non-deceptive and arises from the wisdom realizing that the inherently existent 'I' and 'mine' do not exist. Their realization of divine pride that spontaneously believes themselves to be Heruka therefore has the power to prevent the ignorance of self-grasping, the root of samsara, from arising.

Things do not exist from their own side. There are no inherently existent 'I', 'mine' and other phenomena; all phenomena exist as mere imputations. Things are imputed upon their basis of imputation by thought. What does 'basis of imputation' mean? For example, the parts of a car are the basis of imputation for the car. The parts of a car are not the car, but there is no car other than its parts. Car is imputed upon its parts by thought. How? Through perceiving any of the parts of the car we naturally develop the thought 'This is the car'. Similarly, our body and mind are not our I or self but are the basis of imputation for our I or self. Our I is imputed upon our body or mind by thought. Through perceiving our body or mind we naturally develop the thought 'I' or 'mine'. Without a basis of imputation things cannot exist; everything depends upon its basis of imputation.

Why is it necessary to change the basis of imputation for our I? As mentioned above, since beginningless time in life after life until now, the basis of imputation for our I has only been contaminated aggregates of body and mind. Because the basis of imputation for our I is contaminated by the poison of self-grasping ignorance, we experience the endless cycle of suffering. To free ourself from suffering permanently we therefore need to change our basis of imputation from contaminated aggregates to uncontaminated aggregates.

How can we change our basis of imputation? In general, we have changed our basis of imputation countless times. In our previous lives we took countless rebirths, and each time the basis of imputation for our I was different. When we took a human rebirth our basis of imputation was a human body and mind, and when we took an animal rebirth our basis of imputation was an animal's body and mind. Even in this life, when we were a baby our basis of imputation was a baby's body and mind, when we were a teenager our basis of imputation was a teenager's body and mind, and when we grow old our basis of imputation will be an old person's body and mind. All these countless bases of imputation are contaminated aggregates. We have never changed our basis of imputation from contaminated to uncontaminated aggregates. Only through relying upon Buddha's Tantric teachings can we accomplish this.

We change our basis of imputation from contaminated to uncontaminated aggregates by training in clear appearance and divine pride. As Buddha explained in his Tantric teachings, first we learn to purify our body and mind by meditating on the emptiness of the body, mind and all other phenomena. Perceiving only emptiness, we then generate ourself as an enlightened Deity such as Heruka. We then learn to perceive clearly our body and mind as Heruka's body and mind, our world as Heruka's Pure Land, and all those around us as enlightened Heroes and Heroines. This is called 'training in clear appearance'. Perceiving our body and mind as the uncontaminated aggregates of Heruka's body and mind, we develop the thought 'I am Buddha Heruka'. We then meditate on this divine pride continually with single-pointed concentration until we gain a deep realization of divine pride that spontaneously believes we are Buddha Heruka. At this time we have changed our basis of imputation from contaminated to uncontaminated aggregates.

If we are normally called John, for example, we should never believe that John is Buddha Heruka, but feel that John disappeared into emptiness before we generated as Buddha Heruka. We then believe that our I, which is imputed upon Heruka's body and mind, is Buddha Heruka. This belief is not a mistaken view, because it arises from wisdom, whereas mistaken views necessarily arise from ignorance. The realization of divine pride arises from wisdom and is a powerful method for accumulating great merit and wisdom.

Even if we have the realization that spontaneously believes that we are Buddha Heruka we should never indicate or declare this to others, as such behaviour is inappropriate in normal society. People will still see us as John and not Heruka, and we also know that John is not Heruka. The realizations of divine pride and clear appearance are inner experiences that have the power to control our delusions, and from which pure actions will naturally develop. There is therefore no basis for us to show inappropriate behaviour; we must continue to engage in our daily activities and communicate with others as normal.

We can practise generation stage Tantra in conjunction with the self-generation sadhana of Buddha Heruka, which is a ritual prayer for accomplishing the attainment of Buddha Heruka. A brief sadhana for self-generation as Heruka, called *Vajra Hero Yoga*, can be found in Appendix IV. A detailed explanation of Heruka self-generation can be found in *Essence of Vajrayana*.

MOST of our problems, new
come from Ignorance.
Wrong Views + leads problems
(I, MINE) SELF-graping —
PRIDE → EGO -MIND

Baso Chökyi Gyaltsän

The Tantra of Completion Stage

Generation stage is like drawing the basic outline of a picture and completion stage is like completing the picture. Whereas the principal objects of generation stage meditation – the mandala and Deities – are generated by correct imagination, the principal objects of completion stage meditation – the channels, drops and winds – already exist within our body and there is no need to generate them through the power of imagination. For this reason completion stage is not a creative yoga.

Completion stage Tantra is defined as an inner realization of learning developed in dependence upon the inner winds entering, abiding and dissolving within the central channel through the force of meditations.

The objects of these meditations are the central channel, the indestructible drop, and the indestructible wind and mind.

THE CENTRAL CHANNEL

The central channel is located exactly midway between the left and right halves of the body, but is closer to the back than the front. Immediately in front of the spine is the life channel, which is quite thick; and in front of this is the central channel. It begins at the point between the eyebrows, from where it ascends in an arch to the crown of the head, and then descends in a straight line to the tip of the sex organ.

The central channel is pale blue on the outside and has four attributes: (1) it is very straight, like the trunk of a plantain tree, (2) inside it is an oily red colour, like pure blood, (3) it is very clear and transparent, like a candle flame, and (4) it is very soft and flexible, like a lotus petal.

Either side of the central channel, with no intervening space, are the right and left channels. The right channel is red in colour and the left is white. The right channel begins at the tip of the right nostril and the left channel at the tip of the left nostril. From there, they both ascend in an arch to the crown of the head, either side of the central channel. From the crown of the head down to the navel, these three main channels are straight and adjacent to one another. As the left channel continues down below the level of the navel, it curves a little to the right, separating slightly from the central channel and rejoining it at the tip of the sex organ. There it functions to hold and release sperm, blood and urine. As the right channel continues down below the level of the navel, it curves a little to the left and terminates at the tip of the anus, where it functions to hold and release faeces and so forth.

The right and left channels coil around the central channel at various places, thereby forming the so-called 'channel knots'. The four places at which these knots occur are, in ascending order: the navel channel wheel, or navel chakra, the heart channel wheel, the throat channel wheel and the crown channel wheel. At each of these places, except at the heart, there is a twofold knot formed by a single coil of the right channel and a single coil of the left. As the right and left channels ascend to these places, they coil around the central channel by crossing in front and then looping around it. They then continue upward to the level of the next knot. At the heart level, the same thing happens, except that here there is a sixfold knot formed by three overlapping loops of each of the flanking channels. The channels are the paths through which the inner winds and drops flow. To begin with, it is sufficient simply to become familiar with the description and visualization of the three channels. A more detailed explanation of channels can be found in Appendix II.

THE INDESTRUCTIBLE DROP

There are two types of drop in the body: white drops and red drops. The former are the pure essence of white seminal fluid or sperm, and the latter are the pure essence of blood. Both have gross and subtle forms. The white and red drops that flow outside the central channel are gross drops. The central channel contains both gross and subtle drops.

The principal seat of the white drop (also known as 'white bodhichitta') is the crown channel wheel, and it is from here that the white seminal fluid originates. The principal seat of the red drop (also known as 'red bodhichitta') is the navel channel wheel, and it is from here that the blood originates. The red drop at the navel is also the foundation of the warmth of the body and the basis for attaining inner fire, or tummo, realizations. When the drops melt and flow through the channels, they give rise to an experience of bliss.

As just explained, at the heart channel wheel there is a sixfold knot formed by the right and left channels coiling around the central channel and constricting it. This is the most difficult knot to loosen, but when it is loosened through meditation we shall develop great power – the realization of clear light. Because the central channel at the heart is constricted by this sixfold knot, it is blocked like a tube of bamboo. Inside the central channel, at the very centre of this sixfold knot, is a small vacuole, and inside this is a drop called the 'indestructible drop'. It is the size of a small pea, with the upper half white in colour and the lower half red. The substance of the white half is the very clear essence of sperm, and the substance of the red half is the very clear essence of blood. This drop, which is very pure and subtle, is the very essence of all drops. All the ordinary red and white drops throughout the body originally come from this drop.

The indestructible drop is like a small pea that has been cut in half, slightly hollowed out, and then rejoined. It is called the 'indestructible drop' because its two halves never separate until death. When we die, all the inner winds dissolve into the indestructible drop, and this causes the drop to open. As the two halves separate, our consciousness immediately leaves our body and goes to the next life.

THE INDESTRUCTIBLE WIND AND MIND

The nature of the indestructible wind is a very subtle 'inner wind'. Inner winds are energy winds that flow through the channels of the body, and they are much more subtle than outer winds. They are associated with, and act as mounts for, various minds. Without these winds our mind cannot move from one object to another. It is said that inner winds are like someone who is blind but who has legs because they cannot perceive anything but can move from one place to another. Minds are like someone who has eyes but no legs because minds can see but cannot move without their mount, the inner winds. Because minds are always mounted upon their associated inner winds, they can both see and move.

Inner winds that flow through the left and right channels are impure and harmful because they act as mounts for the minds of self-grasping, self-cherishing and other delusions. We need to make great effort to bring and dissolve these inner winds into the central channel so that we can prevent these delusions from arising.

For ordinary beings, inner winds enter, abide and dissolve within the central channel only during the death process and deep sleep. At these times the indestructible wind and mind manifest, but ordinary beings cannot recognize

Drubchen Dharmavajra

them because their memory or mindfulness is unable to function then. Completion stage Tantric practitioners can cause their inner winds to enter, abide and dissolve within the central channel at any time through the power of their meditation on the channels, drops and winds. They can therefore accomplish the realizations of the five stages of completion stage Tantra: (1) the initial realization of spontaneous great bliss (isolated body and speech of completion stage), (2) ultimate example clear light, (3) illusory body, (4) meaning clear light, and (5) the union of meaning clear light and the pure illusory body. From the fifth stage, practitioners will attain actual enlightenment within a few months.

There are five root and five branch winds. The root winds are:

1 The life-supporting wind
2 The downward-voiding wind
3 The upward-moving wind
4 The equally-abiding wind
5 The pervading wind

The five branch winds are:

6 The moving wind
7 The intensely-moving wind
8 The perfectly-moving wind
9 The strongly-moving wind
10 The definitely-moving wind

A detailed explanation of inner winds can be found in Appendix III.

The indestructible wind is the very subtle wind that is associated with, and acts as the mount for, the very subtle mind. It is called the 'continuously residing body' because we have had this body continuously in life after life. Although our mind of self-cherishing believes that our present body is our own body and cherishes it, in reality our present body is a part of others' bodies because it is part of our parents' bodies. Our I or self imputed upon our present body and mind will cease at the end of the death process, whereas our I imputed upon our continuously residing body and mind will never cease, but goes from one life to the next. It is this person or I that will finally become an enlightened being. Through this we can understand that, according to Highest Yoga Tantra, in the mental continuum of each and every living being there is a deathless person or I who possesses a deathless body. However, without relying upon the profound instructions of Highest Yoga Tantra we cannot recognize our own deathless body and deathless I, our actual self. A Yogi once said:

First, due to fear of death, I ran towards Dharma.
Then I trained in the state of deathlessness.
Finally I realized there is no death and I relaxed!

Inside the indestructible drop resides the indestructible wind and mind, the union of our very subtle wind and very subtle mind. The very subtle wind is our own body, or continuously residing body. The very subtle mind, or indestructible mind, is our own mind, or continuously residing mind, and is mounted upon the very subtle wind. Because the union of our very subtle wind and very subtle mind never ceases, it is called the 'indestructible wind and mind'. Our indestructible wind and mind have never separated since beginningless time, and they will never separate in the future. The potential to communicate possessed by the combination of our very subtle body and mind is our very subtle speech, which is our own speech, or continuously residing speech. This will become a Buddha's speech in the future. In short, inside the indestructible drop is our own body, speech and mind, which in the future will become the enlightened body, speech and mind of a Buddha.

Having gained some experience of generation stage Tantra, which is like drawing the basic outline of a picture, we need to engage in the meditations on completion stage Tantra in order to complete the picture. These are the meditations on the central channel, indestructible drop, and indestructible wind and mind, known as the 'yogas of the channel, drop and wind'. We should engage in these meditations continually with the practice of the preliminary guide, which will be explained in Part Two.

HOW TO MEDITATE ON THE CENTRAL CHANNEL

First, we should learn to perceive what our central channel looks like, contemplating as follows:

My central channel is located exactly midway between the left and right halves of my body, but is closer to the back than the front. Immediately in front of the spine, there is the life channel, which is quite thick; and in front of this is the central channel. It begins at the point between my eyebrows, from where it ascends in an arch to the crown of my head, and then descends in a straight line to the tip of my sex organ. It is pale blue in colour on the outside, and it is an oily red colour on the inside. It is clear and transparent, and very soft and flexible.

At the very beginning we can, if we wish, visualize the central channel as being fairly wide, and then gradually visualize it as being thinner and thinner until finally we are able to visualize it as being the width of a drinking straw. We contemplate like this repeatedly until we perceive a generic image of our central channel. Believing that our mind is inside the central channel at our heart, we focus single-pointedly on the central channel at the level of our heart and meditate on this. We should train continually in this way until we gain deep experience of this meditation.

HOW TO MEDITATE ON THE INDESTRUCTIBLE DROP

To perceive our indestructible drop, we contemplate as follows:

Inside my central channel at the level of my heart there is a small vacuole. Inside this is my indestructible drop. It is the size of a small pea, with the upper half white in colour and the lower half red. It is like a pea that has been cut in half, slightly hollowed out, and then rejoined. It is the very essence of all drops and is very pure and subtle. Even though it is the substance of blood and sperm, it has a very clear nature, like a tiny ball of crystal that radiates five-coloured rays of light.

We contemplate like this repeatedly until we perceive a clear generic image of our indestructible drop at our heart inside our central channel. With the feeling that our mind is inside our indestructible drop at our heart, we meditate on this drop single-pointedly without distraction.

This meditation is a powerful method for causing our inner winds to enter, abide and dissolve within the central channel. Master Ghantapa said:

We should meditate single-pointedly
On the indestructible drop that always abides at our
  heart.
Those who are familiar with this meditation
Will definitely develop exalted wisdom.

Here 'exalted wisdom' means the wisdom of the clear light of bliss experienced when the knots at the heart channel wheel are loosened. Of all the knots in the central channel, these are the most difficult to loosen; but if from the beginning of our completion stage practice we concentrate on our heart channel wheel, this will help us to loosen these knots. This meditation, therefore, is a powerful method for gaining qualified completion stage realizations.

HOW TO MEDITATE ON THE INDESTRUCTIBLE
WIND AND MIND

To gain deeper experience of the wisdom of the clear light of bliss, we engage in meditation on the indestructible wind and mind. First we find the object of this meditation, that is, the clear perception of our indestructible wind and mind, by contemplating as follows:

The nada
(reproduced to the size at which it should be visualized)

Inside my indestructible drop is the union of my indestructible wind and mind in the aspect of a tiny nada, which symbolizes Heruka's mind of clear light. It is reddish-white in colour and radiates five–coloured rays of light. My indestructible drop, located inside my central channel at my heart, is like a house and the union of my indestructible wind and mind is like someone living inside this house.

We contemplate repeatedly in this way until we perceive the nada, which is the nature of the union of our indestructible wind and mind. With the strong recognition that the nada is the union of our very subtle wind and mind, and feeling that our mind has entered into this nada, we meditate single-pointedly on the nada without forgetting it.

Through gaining deep experience of the meditations on the central channel, the indestructible drop, and the union of the indestructible wind and mind, our inner winds will enter, abide and dissolve within the central channel, and we shall experience special signs. We can tell whether or not the winds have entered the central channel by checking our breathing. Normally there are imbalances in our breath – more air is exhaled through one nostril than through the other, and the air begins to leave one nostril before the other. However, when the winds have entered the central channel as a result of the meditations explained above, the pressure and the timing of the breath will be the same for both nostrils during inhalation and exhalation. Therefore, the first sign to be noticed is that we will be breathing evenly through both nostrils. Another noticeable imbalance in the normal breath is that the inhalation is stronger than the exhalation, or vice versa. The second sign that the winds have entered the central channel is that the pressure of the inhalation will be exactly equal to that of the exhalation.

There are also two signs indicating that the winds are abiding in the central channel: (1) our breathing becomes weaker and weaker, eventually ceasing completely, and (2) all abdominal movement normally associated with the breath stops. In the normal course of events, if our breathing were to stop we would be filled with panic and think that we were close to death, but if we are able to stop breathing through the force of meditation, far from panicking our mind will become even more confident, comfortable and flexible.

When the winds are abiding within the central channel, we no longer have to rely upon gross air to survive. Normally our breathing stops only at the time of death. During sleep our breathing becomes much more subtle, but it never stops completely. During completion stage meditation, however, our breath can come to a complete halt without our becoming unconscious. After the winds have been abiding in the central channel for five or ten minutes, it is possible that they will escape again into the right and left channels. If this happens, we shall resume breathing. Air flowing through the nostrils is an indication that the winds are not abiding within the central channel.

What are the signs that the winds have dissolved within the central channel? There are seven winds that must dissolve, and each has a specific sign indicating that its dissolution has been completed. The seven winds are:

1 The earth element wind
2 The water element wind
3 The fire element wind
4 The wind element wind
5 The wind mounted by the mind of white appearance
6 The wind mounted by the mind of red increase
7 The wind mounted by the mind of black near-attainment

The first four of these winds are gross and the last three are subtle. These seven winds dissolve gradually in sequence, and with each dissolution there is a particular appearance.

The earth element wind supports and increases everything that is associated with the earth element in our body, such as our bones, cartilage and fingernails. When this wind dissolves within the central channel, we perceive an appearance known as the 'mirage-like appearance'. This is like the appearance of shimmering water that is sometimes seen on the floor of a desert. There are three levels on which this mirage-like appearance is perceived, depending upon the degree to which the earth element wind has dissolved within the central channel. If the dissolution is only slight the appearance will be vague, the least clear, and very difficult to recognize; if the dissolution is almost complete the appearance will be clearer and more vivid; and if the wind dissolves completely the appearance will be unmistakenly clear and vivid, and impossible not to perceive. When the earth element wind has dissolved and the mirage-like appearance has been perceived, the next wind will dissolve and a different appearance will manifest. The more completely the first wind dissolves, the more vivid will be our perception of this next appearance.

The second wind to dissolve is the water element wind, which supports and increases the liquid elements of the body such as the blood. The appearance associated with this dissolution is called the 'smoke-like appearance'. Some texts say that this appearance is like smoke billowing from a chimney, but this is not the actual appearance. There is an appearance like billowing smoke, but this occurs just prior to the actual dissolution of the water element wind. It is not until this initial appearance has subsided that the actual smoke-like appearance is perceived. This is like thin wisps of wafting blue smoke drifting in the air in a slowly swirling haze. As before, there are three levels on which this appearance is perceived, depending upon the degree to which the water element has dissolved.

Next comes the dissolution of the fire element wind. This wind supports and increases the fire element in the body and is responsible for bodily heat and so forth. The sign that this wind has dissolved is the 'sparkling-fireflies-like appearance'. This appearance is sometimes described in terms of an open crackling fire seen at night, with the mass of ascending sparks swirling above the fire resembling the sparkling-fireflies-like appearance. Once again, there are three levels on which this appearance is perceived, depending upon the degree of dissolution.

Following this, the wind element wind dissolves. This is the wind mounted by gross conceptual thought. It powers gross dualistic appearances and the gross conceptual thoughts that result from holding these appearances to be true. The sign that the fourth of the gross winds has started to dissolve is the 'candle-flame-like appearance'. This is like the steady, erect flame of a candle in a draughtless room. Once again there are three levels on which this appearance is perceived.

When the earth element wind has dissolved within the central channel and the power of the earth element is thereby diminished, it may seem as though the water element has increased because, as the power of the former element diminishes, the latter is perceived more clearly. For this reason, the dissolution of the earth element wind into the central channel is often described as 'the earth element dissolving into the water element'. For similar reasons, the subsequent dissolutions are referred to as 'the water element dissolving into the fire element', 'the fire element dissolving into the wind element', and 'the wind element dissolving into consciousness'.

After the candle-flame-like appearance, all gross conceptual minds have ceased functioning because the winds upon which they are mounted have dissolved and disappeared. When the meditator has completed the dissolution of the fourth wind, the first subtle mind – the mind of white appearance – arises. With this mind, the meditator perceives an appearance of whiteness, like the bright light of the moon pervading an empty sky on a clear autumn night. As before, there are three levels of clarity to this appearance depending upon the ability of the meditator.

At this point the mind is completely free from gross conceptions, such as the eighty indicative conceptions listed in

Gyalwa Ensäpa

Clear Light of Bliss, and the only perception is that of white, empty space. Ordinary beings also perceive this appearance, for example at the time of death, but they are unable to recognize it or to prolong it because at this stage the ordinary gross level of mindfulness has ceased to function. However, even though there is no gross mindfulness at this stage, those who have trained properly according to the practices of completion stage Tantra are able to use the subtle mindfulness they have developed during meditation to recognize and prolong the white appearance, something that ordinary beings are unable to do.

When the subtle wind mounted by the mind of white appearance dissolves, the mind of red increase arises. This mind and its mounted wind are more subtle than the mind and wind of white appearance. The sign that occurs when this mind arises is an appearance like red sunlight pervading an empty sky. Once again, there are three levels of clarity to this appearance.

When the subtle wind mounted by the mind of red increase dissolves, the mind of black near-attainment arises. This mind and its mounted wind are even more subtle than the mind and wind of red increase. The mind of black near-attainment has two levels: the upper part and the lower part. The upper part of the mind of black near-attainment still possesses subtle mindfulness, but the lower part has no mindfulness at all. It is experienced as an overwhelming unconsciousness, like that of a very deep faint. At this point, we would appear to others to be dead.

The sign that occurs when the mind of black near-attainment arises is an appearance like a very black, empty sky. This appearance comes with the upper part of the mind of black near-attainment, immediately after the cessation of the mind of red increase. As the experience of black near-attainment progresses and we approach complete unconsciousness our subtle mindfulness ceases. The more strongly the wind dissolves into the central channel, the more deeply unconscious we become during the mind of black near-attainment; and the more deeply unconscious we become at this time, the more vividly we shall perceive the subsequent appearance of clear light. This is similar to the experience of someone who stays in a dark room for a long time; the longer he stays there, the brighter the outside world will appear when he eventually emerges. Thus, the degree of brightness experienced depends upon the depth and duration of the previous darkness.

When the subtle wind mounted by the mind of black near-attainment dissolves, the mind of clear light arises. This mind and its mounted wind are the most subtle of all. The sign that occurs when this mind arises is an appearance like an autumn sky at dawn – perfectly clear and empty.

When the mind of clear light arises, a very subtle mindfulness is restored, according to the meditator's level of development. The very subtle wind and the very subtle mind that is mounted upon it reside in the indestructible drop in the centre of the heart channel wheel. Normally the very subtle mind does not function, but at the time of the clear light it manifests and becomes active. If we have trained in the techniques of completion stage Tantra, and have become proficient in them, we shall be able to perceive and maintain the appearance of clear light. Eventually, by learning to use the very subtle mindfulness developed at this stage, we shall be able to focus our very subtle mind on emptiness, and in this way use the mind of clear light as the means for attaining a Buddha's Truth Body.

Our mind cannot become more subtle than the mind of clear light. During the first four appearances (mirage-like, smoke-like, sparkling-fireflies-like and candle-flame-like) the gross winds dissolve; and during the next three (white appearance, red increase and black near-attainment) the subtle winds dissolve. Then, with the appearance of the clear light, the very subtle mind and its mounted wind manifest and become active. These cannot dissolve because they are indestructible. After death, they simply pass to the next life.

Of the three subtle winds mounted by the three subtle minds, the least subtle is that mounted by the mind of white appearance. This mind is called 'white appearance' because all that is perceived is an appearance of white, empty space. It is also called 'empty' because the mind of white appearance perceives this white space as empty. At this stage the appearance of white and the appearance of empty are of equal strength.

When the wind mounted by the mind of white appearance dissolves, the second of the three subtle minds – the mind of red increase – arises. The mounted wind of this mind is more subtle than that mounted by the mind of white appearance. This mind is called 'red increase' because the appearance of red space is increasing. It is also called 'very empty' because the appearance of empty is stronger than that of the previous mind. At this stage the appearance of empty is stronger than the appearance of red.

When the wind of the mind of red increase dissolves, the third subtle mind – the mind of black near-attainment – arises. This mind is called 'near-attainment' because the experience of clear light is now close at hand. It is also called 'great empty' because the appearance of empty is even greater than that of the previous mind.

When the third subtle wind, that mounted by the mind of black near-attainment, dissolves, the mind of clear light arises. This mind is called 'clear light' because its nature is very lucid and clear, and because it perceives an appearance like the light of an autumn dawn. It is also called 'all-empty' because it is empty of all gross and subtle winds and perceives only an empty appearance. The object of the mind of clear light is very similar in appearance to the object perceived by a Superior being in meditative equipoise on emptiness. Collectively, the four minds – the mind of white appearance, the mind of red increase, the mind of black near-attainment, and the mind of clear light – are referred to as the 'four empties'.

If a completion stage meditator is highly accomplished, he or she will have a very vivid experience of clear light and will be able to maintain that experience for a long time. Just how vivid our experience of clear light is depends upon how vivid the previous seven appearances were, and this in turn depends upon how strongly the winds dissolve within the central channel. If the winds dissolve very strongly, the meditator will have a vivid experience of all the appearances and will be able to prolong the experience of each one. The longer we are able to remain with the experience of each appearance, the longer we shall be able to remain with the clear light itself.

If a person dies a violent death, he or she progresses through these appearances very rapidly, but if the death is slow or natural the appearances from mirage-like to clear light will be experienced more gradually and for longer. If we have developed the realization of ultimate example clear light, we shall be able to have exactly the same experience of these appearances while in deep concentration that we would have if we were actually dying. Moreover, if we have trained well in the meditations explained above, we shall be able to meditate on emptiness throughout all four empties, except during the time spent in the swoon, or faint, of the mind of black near-attainment.

To be able to perceive the four empties clearly, exactly as in the death process, we must be able to dissolve all the winds into the indestructible drop in the centre of the heart channel wheel. If they dissolve into another channel wheel of the central channel, such as the navel channel wheel, we shall experience similar appearances, but they will be artificial – not the true appearances that occur when the winds dissolve into the indestructible drop, as they do at the time of death.

Although an accomplished meditator can abide within the clear light for a long time, he or she must eventually move on. When we arise from the clear light, the first thing we experience is the mind of black near-attainment of reverse order. Then we experience in sequence the mind of red increase, the mind of white appearance, the eighty gross conceptual minds, the minds of the candle-flame-like appearance and so forth, as the minds evolve in an order that is the reverse of that in which they previously dissolved.

Thus the mind of clear light is the foundation of all other minds. When the gross and subtle minds and their mounted winds dissolve into the indestructible drop at the heart, we remain with only the clear light, and then it is from this clear light that all the other minds evolve, each one grosser than the previous one.

These sequences of serial and reverse order are experienced by ordinary beings during death and the initial stages of their next rebirth and by qualified completion stage practitioners during meditation. Because enlightened beings have attained permanent cessation of the seven winds listed above, they experience only the very subtle mind of clear light – even their compassion and bodhichitta are part of their mind of clear light.

What is Mahamudra?

The term 'Mahamudra' is Sanskrit. 'Maha' means 'great' and refers to great bliss, and 'mudra' here means 'non-deceptive' and refers to emptiness. Mahamudra is the union of great bliss and emptiness. Mahamudra Tantra is defined as a mind of fully qualified clear light that experiences great bliss and realizes emptiness directly. Because emptiness is explained in detail in Buddha's Sutra teachings and is a part of Mahamudra, some texts say that it is Sutra Mahamudra, but actual Mahamudra is necessarily a realization of Highest Yoga Tantra.

Mahamudra is the very essence of Buddha's teachings. Because the teachings of Je Tsongkhapa Losang Dragpa – the manifestation of the Wisdom Buddha – give clear and unmistaken instructions on Mahamudra Tantra, in *Prayer for the Flourishing of the Doctrine of Je Tsongkhapa* the scholar Guntang says:

Khädrub Sangye Yeshe

The emptiness that is explained in Buddha's Sutra
   teachings,
And the great bliss that is explained in Buddha's
   Tantric teachings –
The union of these two is the very essence of
   Buddha's eighty-four thousand teachings.
May the doctrine of Conqueror Losang Dragpa
   flourish for evermore.

The nature of Mahamudra is a fully qualified clear light. As mentioned previously there are many different levels of the experience of clear light depending upon the degree of dissolution of the inner winds into the central channel. The realization of great bliss developed in dependence upon the inner winds entering, abiding and dissolving within the central channel, prior to attaining the fully qualified clear light, is the first of the five stages of completion stage. It is called 'isolated body and speech of completion stage', which means that at this stage the practitioner is free, or isolated, from gross ordinary appearances and conceptions of body and speech.

A fully qualified clear light mind experiencing great bliss that realizes emptiness with a generic image is called 'ultimate example clear light'. This realization is called 'ultimate' because it is a fully qualified clear light. It is called 'example' because by using this realization as an example, practitioners understand that they can accomplish a fully qualified clear light mind experiencing great bliss that realizes emptiness directly, which is called 'meaning clear light'. The realization of ultimate example clear light is the second of the five stages of completion stage. It is also called 'isolated mind' because at this stage practitioners are free, or isolated, from gross ordinary appearances and conceptions of mind.

When practitioners arise from the concentration of ultimate example clear light, their indestructible wind – their continuously residing body – transforms into the illusory body. This is a divine body, which in nature is wisdom light having the aspect of the divine body of an enlightened Deity such as Heruka. The colour of the illusory body is white. The realization of this illusory body is the third of the five stages of completion stage, and is called 'illusory body of the third stage'.

Practitioners who have attained the illusory body of the third stage meditate on emptiness again and again with their clear light mind of bliss until they directly realize the emptiness of all phenomena. When they accomplish this they attain 'meaning clear light', a fully qualified clear light mind experiencing great bliss that realizes the emptiness of all phenomena directly. This realization of meaning clear light is the fourth of the five stages of completion stage, and is called 'meaning clear light of the fourth stage'. 'Meaning clear light' and 'Mahamudra Tantra' are synonymous.

When practitioners arise from the concentration of meaning clear light they attain the pure illusory body and completely abandon ordinary conceptions and all other delusions. When these practitioners manifest meaning clear light again, they will attain the union of meaning clear light and pure illusory body. The realization of this union is the fifth of the five stages of completion stage, and is called 'union of the fifth stage'. From this fifth stage practitioners will attain actual enlightenment – the Path of No More Learning, or Buddhahood.

As mentioned above, Mahamudra is the union of great bliss and emptiness. This means that Mahamudra Tantra is a single mind that is both bliss and wisdom: it experiences great bliss and realizes emptiness directly. Mahamudra Tantra is a collection of merit that is the main cause of a Buddha's Form Body, and a collection of wisdom that is the main cause of a Buddha's Truth Body, or Dharmakaya. When training in the meditations of Mahamudra Tantra we are transforming our continuously residing body and mind into a Buddha's Form Body and Truth Body. Mahamudra Tantra, therefore, gives inconceivable meaning to our life.

GREAT BLISS

The bliss explained by Buddha in completion stage Tantra is unequalled among all other types of bliss and is therefore called 'great bliss'.

In general, there are many different types of bliss. For example, ordinary beings sometimes experience some artificial bliss when they engage in sexual activity, and qualified meditators experience a special bliss of suppleness during deep meditation due to their pure concentration, especially when they attain tranquil abiding and accomplish the concentration of the absorption of cessation. Moreover when Dharma practitioners, through training in higher moral discipline, higher concentration and higher wisdom, attain permanent inner peace by abandoning self-grasping, they experience a profound bliss of inner peace day and night in life after life. These types of bliss are mentioned in Buddha's Sutra teachings. The bliss of completion stage, however, is quite different from all of these, and is vastly superior. The bliss of completion stage – great bliss – is a bliss that possesses two special characteristics: (1) its nature is a bliss arisen from the melting of the drops inside the central channel, and (2) its function is to overcome ordinary or dualistic appearance. No other form of bliss possesses these two characteristics.

A bliss possessing these two characteristics can be experienced only by human beings who are engaged in Highest Yoga Tantra practice, and by Buddhas. Even high Bodhisattvas abiding in Pure Lands have no opportunity to experience it because, even though they have very high realizations, their bodies lack the necessary physical conditions for generating bliss possessing the two characteristics. What are these conditions? They are the three elements of flesh, skin and blood that come from the mother; and the three elements of bone, marrow and sperm that come from the father. These six elements are essential for accomplishing this bliss, which is the quick path to Buddhahood. It was because humans possessed these conditions that Buddha explained Tantric teachings to us in the first place. Therefore, from this point of view, we are more fortunate than high Bodhisattvas abiding in Pure Lands who are experiencing great enjoyments. It is said that these Bodhisattvas pray to be born in the human world so that they can meet a qualified Vajra Master and practise the quick path to enlightenment. In *Song of the Spring Queen*, Je Tsongkhapa says that without experiencing this bliss there is no possibility of attaining liberation in this life. It goes without saying, therefore, that without this bliss there is no possibility of attaining full enlightenment in this life.

If we develop and maintain this bliss through the practice of completion stage meditation, we can transform our attachment into a special method for completing the quick path to enlightenment. Before we attain this bliss, our attachment causes us to be reborn in samsara, but once we have this bliss our attachment causes us to be released from samsara. Moreover, once we attain this bliss we shall be able to stop our samsaric rebirths very quickly. The cause of samsara is our mind of self-grasping. According to the teachings of Highest Yoga Tantra, self-grasping depends upon its mounted wind, which flows through the right and left channels. For human beings, without this wind self-grasping cannot develop. By gaining the bliss of completion stage, we can gradually reduce the inner winds of the right and left channels until finally they cease completely. When they cease, our self-grasping ceases, and we experience liberation from samsara.

From this we can see that in Sutra alone there is no liberation, not to mention full enlightenment. The Highest Yoga Tantra teachings are Buddha's ultimate intention, and the Sutra teachings are like the basic foundation. Although there are many explanations of how to attain liberation or nirvana in the Sutra teachings, if we check precisely it is very difficult to understand from Sutra teachings how nirvana can be attained. 'Nirvana' means 'the state beyond sorrow' – the permanent cessation of self-grasping and its

Panchen Losang Chökyi Gyaltsän

mounted wind – and its nature is emptiness. If we have never heard Tantric teachings and someone asks us precisely how we attain such a nirvana, we cannot give a perfect answer. As Je Tsongkhapa said, the final answer can be found only in the Tantric teachings.

The bliss that arises from the melting of drops inside channels other than the central channel has no special qualities. When ordinary beings engage in sexual intercourse, for example, this causes their downward-voiding wind to move upwards, and this in turn causes their ordinary inner heat, or tummo, to increase in their right and left channels, principally in the left. As a result the red drops of the woman and the white drops of the man melt and flow through the left channel. This flowing of the drops causes them to experience some bliss, but it is very short-lived and the drops are soon released. Having had this brief experience of bliss, they are not left with any good results, except maybe a baby!

By contrast, when a qualified Tantric practitioner practises the completion stage meditations that are explained above, he or she will cause his inner winds to gather, abide and dissolve within the central channel. This will cause the downward-voiding wind located just below the navel to move upwards. Normally this wind functions to release the drops, but because it is now rising within the central channel, the inner heat located at the navel will increase inside the central channel, thereby causing the drops to melt and flow also inside the central channel.

For the practitioner of a male Deity, the white drop begins to flow down from the crown and, when it reaches the throat, the practitioner experiences a very special bliss possessing the two characteristics, or qualities. As the drop flows down to the heart, the bliss becomes stronger and more qualified; as it flows down to the navel, the bliss becomes even stronger and more qualified; and finally, as it flows down to the tip of the sex organ, the practitioner experiences spontaneous great bliss – the great bliss of completion stage. Because the downward-voiding wind is reversed, the drop is not released at this point but flows up again through the central channel, causing the practitioner to experience even greater bliss. For such a practitioner, the drops are never released and so they flow up and down the central channel for a very long time, giving rise to unceasing bliss. The practitioner can cause such bliss to manifest at any time simply by penetrating the central channel with concentration.

The stronger this bliss becomes, the more subtle our mind becomes. Gradually our mind becomes very peaceful, all conceptual distractions disappear, and we experience very special suppleness. This mind is infinitely superior to the experience of tranquil abiding explained in Sutra teachings. Moreover, as our mind becomes more subtle our dualistic appearance is reduced, and eventually our mind becomes the very subtle mind of the clear light of bliss. This is a very high realization. When the clear light of bliss concentrates on emptiness it mixes with emptiness very easily because dualistic appearance is greatly reduced. Finally it realizes emptiness directly, and whereas previously it felt as if our bliss and emptiness were two things, now they have become one nature. This mind is the union of great bliss and emptiness, or meaning clear light.

The first moment of the realization of the union of great bliss and emptiness is the path of seeing of Highest Yoga Tantra. However, even though it is only the path of seeing, it has the power to eliminate both the intellectually-formed delusions and innate delusions together. In the second moment, when the practitioner rises from this concentration of the union of bliss and emptiness, he or she has abandoned all the delusions and has attained liberation. At the same time, he or she has attained the pure illusory body. From that moment, the practitioner's body is a vajra body, and so he or she will not have to experience ageing, sickness or death.

As mentioned above, previously when the practitioner was ordinary, he or she was using a body taken from others – from his or her parents. We normally say 'My body, my body' as if our gross body belongs to us, yet this is not our actual body but one that we have taken from others. When a Tantric practitioner attains a vajra body, however, he has manifested his own body, and when he perceives this vajra body he thinks 'I'. Such a practitioner has now become a deathless person.

We have had our very subtle body, very subtle speech and very subtle mind since beginningless time. These are the continuously residing body, the continuously residing speech and the continuously residing mind, and they are our actual Buddha nature. The Buddha nature explained in Sutra is not actual Buddha nature because it is a gross object that will cease; actual Buddha nature is explained only in

Highest Yoga Tantra. Normally, for ordinary beings, the only times their very subtle body, speech and mind become manifest are during deep sleep and death. However, even though they are not normally manifest, our very subtle body is the seed of a Buddha's body, our very subtle speech is the seed of a Buddha's speech, and our very subtle mind is the seed of a Buddha's mind.

As already mentioned, the very subtle body is the very subtle wind upon which the very subtle mind is mounted. This very subtle body and very subtle mind are always together. Since they are the same nature, and are never separated, they are called the 'indestructible wind' and the 'indestructible mind'. The union of the indestructible wind and mind is normally located inside the indestructible drop, inside the central channel at the heart.

Our very subtle mind manifests only when all our inner winds dissolve within our central channel. When this happens we gradually experience the eight signs described previously, as we pass through the different levels of dissolution. Finally, with the last level of dissolution, the very subtle mind of clear light becomes manifest. At the same time, the very subtle body also becomes manifest.

During death, the inner winds dissolve naturally and fully within the central channel and the very subtle mind and very subtle body naturally become manifest, but we cannot recognize them. However, by practising the completion stage meditations explained above, we can cause our very subtle mind and body to become manifest during meditation. Until we attain the realization of illusory body, our very subtle body will not maintain a definite shape or colour. When we attain the union of bliss and emptiness, our very subtle mind transforms into meaning clear light and, when we rise from that meditation, our very subtle body transforms into the vajra body, or pure illusory body, which does have definite shape, colour and so forth.

For example, if we are a Heruka practitioner, whenever we do self-generation as Heruka with a blue-coloured body, four faces, twelve arms and so on, we are building the basic foundation for the illusory body. In the future, when our very subtle body transforms into the illusory body it will look like real Heruka. Previously it was merely an imagined body, but at this time it will become real. This is a very good reason for now practising generation stage very sincerely.

When we attain the pure illusory body, we shall no longer think of our gross body as our body. The basis for imputing our I will have completely changed, and we shall now impute I in dependence upon our subtle body. When we have reached this attainment, we shall have become deathless because our body and mind will never separate. Death is the permanent separation of body and mind, but the body and mind of those who have attained the illusory body never separate because they are indestructible. Finally, our pure illusory body will transform into Buddha's Form Body and our union of bliss and emptiness will transform into Buddha's Truth Body, and we shall experience the union of Buddha's Form Body and Truth Body, the Union of No More Learning.

In the section on the benefits of bodhichitta in *Guide to the Bodhisattva's Way of Life* Shantideva says:

Drubchen Gendun Gyaltsän

Just like the supreme elixir that transmutes into gold,
Bodhichitta can transform this impure body we have
   taken
Into the priceless jewel of a Buddha's form;
Therefore, firmly maintain bodhichitta.

Here, 'elixir' refers to a special substance that can transform iron into gold, like that used by great Masters such as Nagarjuna. This verse says that bodhichitta is a special method that, like a supreme elixir, has the power to transform our impure body into a Buddha's Form Body. How can it do this? According to Sutra, a practitioner cannot attain enlightenment in one life but must practise for many lives until finally he or she is born into Akanishta Pure Land with a pure body. It is only with this pure body that he or she can attain Buddhahood. There is no method in either Sutra or Tantra for transforming our present impure body into a Buddha's body. This impure body must eventually die; it must be left behind. Even the holy Buddha Shakyamuni himself left behind the gross body that came from his parents when he passed away. Thus, if we ask how bodhichitta can transform this impure body into a Buddha's body, there is no correct answer within Sutra teachings. This is because, according to Sutra teachings, the gross body is the real body; the Sutras never mention the vajra body, or the subtle body.

By following the Tantric view, however, we can answer this question as follows. The body referred to by Shantideva is not the gross body, but our own body, our continuously residing body, which is the very subtle wind upon which our very subtle mind is mounted. At present this is an impure body because it is obscured by delusions and other obstructions, like a blue sky covered by clouds. These defilements are not the nature of our subtle body, but are temporary defilements. The method for transforming this impure body into a Buddha's Form Body is not conventional bodhichitta, but the ultimate bodhichitta of Highest Yoga Tantra, the union of great bliss and emptiness. This ultimate bodhichitta can directly transform our impure continuously residing body first into the pure illusory body and finally into the Form Body of a Buddha. Since Shantideva himself was a sincere Tantric practitioner, we can be certain that this was his intended meaning.

As mentioned previously, to generate the bliss that possesses two special qualities we need to gather and dissolve our inner winds within our central channel. There are two ways to do this: by penetrating our own body or by penetrating another's body.

We begin by penetrating our own body. Here, the term 'body' refers to our vajra body – our channels, drops and winds – and 'penetrate' to concentrating on our central channel, drops and winds, as already explained. Meditation on the central channel is called the 'yoga of the central channel', meditation on the drops is called the 'yoga of the drop', and meditation on the winds is called the 'yoga of wind'.

Penetrating another's body means relying upon an action mudra, or consort, and engaging in sexual intercourse. However, just penetrating another's body will not bring our inner winds into our central channel if we do not already have experience of and familiarity with the yoga of the central channel, the yoga of the drop and the yoga of wind. Only when we have such experience is it the right time to rely upon an action mudra. This order of practice is very important.

There are only ten doors through which the winds can enter the central channel. They are located along the central channel as follows:

1 The upper tip of the central channel: the point between the eyebrows
2 The lower tip: the tip of the sex organ
3 The centre of the crown channel wheel: located in the apex of the cranium
4 The centre of the throat channel wheel: located near the back of the throat
5 The centre of the heart channel wheel: located between the two breasts
6 The centre of the navel channel wheel
7 The centre of the secret place channel wheel, four finger-widths below the navel
8 The centre of the jewel channel wheel, located in the centre of the sex organ, near its tip
9 The wheel of wind: the centre of the forehead channel wheel
10 The wheel of fire: the centre of the channel wheel located midway between the throat and the heart channel wheels

Just as we can enter a house through any of the doors leading in from the outside, so the winds can enter the central channel through any of these ten doors.

The central channel is in reality one single channel, but it is divided into different sections: the central channel of the crown channel wheel, the central channel of the throat channel wheel, the central channel of the heart channel wheel, the central channel of the navel channel wheel, and so forth. Because there are these different locations, when a practitioner wants to bring his or her winds into the central channel, he or she must choose one of these points at which to concentrate.

In *Clear Light of Bliss,* I explain how to bring the inner winds into the central channel through the sixth of the ten doors, the centre of the navel channel wheel. We do this by visualizing our inner heat inside our navel channel in the aspect of a short-AH and meditating on this. This is a common practice that accords with the tradition of the Six Yogas of Naropa. It was originally explained in *Hevajra Root Tantra* by Buddha Vajradhara, and since then has been used by many Kagyü practitioners such as Milarepa and his disciples, and later by practitioners in Je Tsongkhapa's tradition. However, according to the instructions of the Ganden Oral Lineage there is the uncommon Mahamudra Tantra practice. This is a very special practice of Mahamudra that Je Tsongkhapa received directly from Manjushri, who had received it directly from Buddha. The lineage of this practice was then passed to Togdän Jampäl Gyatso, Baso Chökyi Gyaltsän, Mahasiddha Dharmavajra, and so on. A full list of the lineage Gurus of this special instruction is given in the sadhanas *Great Liberation of the Father* and *Great Liberation of the Mother.* These Spiritual Guides are the close lineage Gurus.

In this Mahamudra Tantra practice, we choose the heart channel wheel from among the ten doors into the central channel. This practice is indicated in the sadhana *Offering to the Spiritual Guide*, which is the uncommon preliminary practice of Mahamudra Tantra according to Je Tsongkhapa's tradition. The sadhana says:

I seek your blessings, O Protector, that you may
place your feet
On the centre of the eight-petalled lotus at my heart,
So that I may manifest within this life
The paths of illusory body, clear light, and union.

These words actually reveal that penetrating the central channel of the heart channel wheel, the indestructible drop and the indestructible wind – the three yogas explained above – are meditations on isolated body. These lead to the meditations on isolated speech and isolated mind, which in turn lead to the meditations on illusory body, meaning clear light, and union.

Because penetrating and concentrating on the indestructible drop at the heart is a powerful method for attaining the realizations of completion stage, Buddha Vajradhara praises this method in *Ambhidana Tantra*, where he says:

Those who meditate on the drop
That always abides at the heart,
Single-pointedly and without change,
Will definitely attain realizations.

Mahasiddha Ghantapa also encouraged us to do this meditation. Therefore, our uncommon Mahamudra Tantra practice begins with meditating on the central channel of the heart channel wheel.

The transmission, teachings and lineage of this uncommon instruction are not possessed by any other tradition. We can see from the list of lineage Gurus that they are all followers of Je Tsongkhapa. Togdän Jampäl Gyatso, Mahasiddha Dharmavajra, Gyalwa Ensäpa, and their many disciples all attained the Mahamudra that is the Union of No More Learning, or Buddhahood, within three years, joyfully and without any difficulties. They entered the path, progressed along it, and completed it within three years.

In ancient times practitioners like Milarepa worked very hard before engaging in retreat. Milarepa experienced so many difficulties, and after entering retreat he spent a long time in very isolated places, but he was a very patient and determined practitioner, like an iron man. Because of this he attained high realizations; otherwise he would have found it very difficult. Why did he have to labour so long and hard when later practitioners such as Mahasiddha Dharmavajra and Gyalwa Ensäpa were able to attain full enlightenment so quickly and easily? The only reason is that the later practitioners received these special instructions of Je Tsongkhapa, which are very simple and very blessed. For them every problem was easily solved, and it was very easy for them to make progress and attain Buddhahood quickly.

It is said that thousands of Je Tsongkhapa's disciples have attained a deathless vajra body – a pure illusory body – without having to engage in hardships as Milarepa did. They all practised very joyfully and smoothly because of the special qualities of these instructions.

PART TWO

How to Train in Mahamudra

Drungpa Tsöndru Gyaltsän

The Preliminary Guide

There is no real meaning in this ordinary human life. Many people who are old or who are very close to dying understand how human life is empty and hollow. Throughout our life we try very hard to accumulate so many things such as wealth and possessions, but finally, without choice, everything that belonged to us passes to others; we can carry nothing with us to our next life. The real meaning of human life is finding and following the correct path to enlightenment, and the supreme correct path to enlightenment is Highest Yoga Tantra, especially Mahamudra Tantra.

The effectiveness of our meditations on Mahamudra Tantra depends upon our accumulating great merit and wisdom, purifying negativities and receiving the special blessings of the Wisdom Buddha. These are the preliminary guides that make our meditations successful.

In particular, sincere practitioners collect a hundred thousand of each of the following four great preliminary guides. These are (1) going for refuge and generating bodhichitta, (2) a special way of relying upon the Spiritual Guide, known as 'Guru yoga', (3) making mandala offerings, and (4) meditation and recitation of Vajrasattva.

There now follows an explanation of how to practise the preliminary guide to Mahamudra practice in conjunction with *Heart Jewel*, which can be found in Appendix V.

GOING FOR REFUGE

Normally we seek refuge in external sources. When peoples' lives are being threatened, for example, they seek refuge in the police. Sometimes of course police can protect people from particular dangers but no police force can give us permanent protection from death. Similarly, when we are seriously ill we seek refuge in doctors. Sometimes of course doctors can cure particular sicknesses but no doctor can give us permanent liberation from sickness. In this impure world there is no real protection from suffering.

Only by gaining Dharma realizations through receiving Buddha's blessings and the help of Sangha – pure spiritual practitioners – can we attain permanent liberation from sickness, death and all other sufferings. Therefore only the Three Precious Jewels – Buddha, Dharma and Sangha – are the actual refuge that permanently protects living beings from suffering. Contemplating this, we make the strong determination to rely sincerely upon the Three Precious Jewels, with the following refuge prayer:

I and all sentient beings until we achieve enlightenment,
Go for refuge to Buddha, Dharma, and Sangha.

With strong faith we should practise refuge every day, but as the great preliminary guide for our Mahamudra practice we can collect a hundred thousand refuge prayers, either throughout our daily life or in retreat. Detailed explanations of refuge practice can be found in *Guide to Dakini Land* and *Joyful Path of Good Fortune*.

GENERATING BODHICHITTA

'Bodhi' means enlightenment and 'chitta' means mind. Bodhichitta is a mind that spontaneously wishes to attain enlightenment, Buddhahood, for the benefit of all living beings. We can generate this supreme good heart with the following prayer:

Through the virtues I collect by giving and other perfections,
May I become a Buddha for the benefit of all.

Generating the supreme good heart of bodhichitta is essential for effective practice of Mahamudra. Detailed explanations of bodhichitta can be found in *Meaningful to Behold* and *Transform Your Life*.

VISUALIZATION

The instructions on the uncommon practice of Mahamudra Tantra were taught by the Wisdom Buddha Manjushri in the *Kadam Emanation Scripture*, and are called the instructions of the 'Ganden Oral Lineage'. According to these instructions we can accumulate great merit and wisdom, purify our negativities and receive the blessings of the Wisdom Buddha by relying upon the assembly of holy beings of Je Tsongkhapa, the manifestation of the Wisdom Buddha. We visualize these holy beings as follows:

In the space before me the wisdom of all the Buddhas appears in the aspect of Je Tsongkhapa – who is in nature my Spiritual Guide – surrounded by thousands of his Bodhisattva disciples who attained the pure illusory body through practising the instructions of the Ganden Oral Lineage.

INVITATION

From the space of the Dharmakaya at the heart of Buddha Maitreya, who is the Lord of the gods of the Joyful Land of Tushita Heaven, his compassion for the living beings of this world billows in the aspect of white clouds, which descend to the space in front of me, just like a ball of wool unravelling with one end of the thread remaining connected to Maitreya's heart. At the same time, Je Tsongkhapa and his Bodhisattva disciples descend to the space in front of me, dissolve into the visualized assembly of Je Tsongkhapa and his Bodhisattva disciples, and become inseparably one.

This way of inviting Je Tsongkhapa and his Bodhisattva disciples is very special because it indicates that, from the space of Buddha Maitreya's Truth Body, or Dharmakaya, clouds of his compassion for all the beings of this world arise; and, as a result, a rain of Dharma teachings continually descends upon all beings through Je Tsongkhapa and his emanations.

According to common appearance one thousand Buddhas will appear in this world. Buddha Shakyamuni was the fourth and Buddha Maitreya will be the fifth. Inviting Je Tsongkhapa and his Bodhisattva disciples in this way creates a special connection with Buddha Maitreya, so that we can meet him and his doctrine directly when he appears in this world.

We then visualize:

At Je Tsongkhapa's heart is Buddha Shakyamuni, and at his heart is the living Buddha Heruka.

This indicates that Je Tsongkhapa is not different from Buddha Shakyamuni and Heruka but is one being – Lama Losang Buddha Heruka (Guru Sumati Buddha Heruka).

Having accomplished this visualization and invitation, we now believe that Lama Losang Buddha Heruka is always present in front of us. We then contemplate the preeminent qualities of Je Tsongkhapa: his nature is the synthesis of all the Buddhas of the past, present and future, and his function is to bestow upon us the wisdom of example clear light and meaning clear light. In this way, we develop and maintain strong faith in Lama Losang Buddha Heruka. By shining the sun of our faith on the snow mountain of Lama Losang Buddha Heruka, his water-like blessings will continually flow down upon us, nourishing and healing our mental continuum.

THE PRACTICE OF THE SEVEN LIMBS

The seven limbs are: (1) requesting the Spiritual Guides to remain for a long time, (2) prostration, (3) offerings, (4) purification, (5) rejoicing, (6) requesting the turning of the

Könchog Gyaltsän

Wheel of Dharma, and (7) dedication. In this context, training in Mahamudra Tantra is like the main body, and the practice of the seven limbs are like the limbs that support it. Just as our body is able to function in dependence upon its limbs, the effectiveness of our training in Mahamudra depends upon our practice of the seven limbs.

REQUESTING THE SPIRITUAL GUIDES TO REMAIN FOR A LONG TIME

In this practice we think:

> *If the Spiritual Teachers who have been emanated by the holy beings remain in this world for many aeons, gradually all living beings will have the opportunity to listen to, understand and practise Dharma. In this way, eventually all living beings, without exception, will attain enlightenment.*

We then make requests to Lama Losang Buddha Heruka, asking that his emanations who are teaching Dharma will remain in this world until samsara ends, while reciting the following verse:

> *In the space before me on a lion throne, lotus, and moon,*
> *The venerable Gurus smile with delight.*
> *O Supreme Field of Merit for my mind of faith,*
> *Please remain for a hundred aeons to spread the doctrine.*

PROSTRATION

Making prostrations to enlightened beings is a powerful method for purifying negative karma, sickness and obstacles, and for increasing our merit, our happiness and our Dharma realizations. Temporarily prostrations improve our physical health and make our mind happy, and ultimately they cause us to attain a Buddha's Form Body. Generating faith in the holy beings is mental prostration, reciting praises to them is verbal prostration, and showing respect to them with our body is physical prostration. We can make physical prostrations by respectfully prostrating our entire body on the ground; by respectfully touching our knees, palms and forehead to the ground; or by respectfully placing our palms together at the level of our heart.

To make powerful prostrations to the holy beings, we imagine that from every pore of our body we emanate another body, and from every pore of these bodies we emanate yet more bodies, until our emanated bodies fill the entire world. Then, while reciting the following verse, we strongly believe that all these countless bodies make prostrations to Lama Losang Buddha Heruka and all the other holy beings:

*Your mind of wisdom realizes the full extent of objects of
 knowledge,*
Your eloquent speech is the ear-ornament of the fortunate,
Your beautiful body is ablaze with the glory of renown,
*I prostrate to you, whom to see, to hear, and to remember
 is so meaningful.*

We should do this practice of prostration every day. As a preliminary guide for our Mahamudra practice, we can collect a hundred thousand prostrations, either throughout our daily life or in retreat.

OFFERINGS

From the depths of our heart we make the following determination:

To liberate all living beings from suffering permanently
I make excellent offerings to the supreme holy being
Lama Losang Buddha Heruka,
And to all the other holy beings.

However many flowers and fruits there are,
And all the different types of medicine;
All the jewels there are in the world,
And all the pure, refreshing waters;

Mountains of jewels, forest groves,
And quiet and joyful places;
Heavenly trees adorned with flowers,
And trees whose branches hang with delicious fruits;

Scents that come from the celestial realms,
Incense, wish-granting trees, and jewelled trees;
Harvests that need no cultivation,
And all ornaments that are suitable to be offered;

Lakes and pools adorned with lotuses,
And the beautiful call of wild geese;
Everything that is unowned
Throughout all worlds as extensive as space –

Holding these in my mind, I offer them well
To you, the supreme beings, the Buddhas and Bodhisattvas.
O Compassionate Ones, holy objects of offering,
Think of me kindly and accept what I offer.

Eternally I will offer all my bodies
To you, the Buddhas and Bodhisattvas.
Out of respect, I will become your servant;
Please accept me, O Supreme Heroes.

While we imagine making all of these offerings, we can
recite the following short verse:

Pleasing water offerings, various flowers,
Sweet-smelling incense, lights, scented water, and so
  forth,
A vast cloud of offerings both set out and imagined,
I offer to you, O Supreme Field of Merit.

In Buddhism an offering is anything that delights the
enlightened beings. Our main offering is our practice of
compassion, as this gives enlightened beings the greatest
delight. Therefore, our motivation for making offerings
should be compassion for all living beings – our sincere
wish to liberate all living beings from suffering permanently.

In summary, we should always regard all our daily
Dharma practices as unsurpassed offerings to Lama Losang
Buddha Heruka – the synthesis of our Spiritual Guide, Je
Tsongkhapa, Buddha Shakyamuni and Heruka – and to all
the other enlightened beings. In this way we can accumu-
late immeasurable merit, or good fortune.

PURIFICATION

Purification is the supreme method to prevent future suffering and to remove obstacles to our Dharma practice, especially to the practice of Mahamudra Tantra. It makes our

actions pure so that we ourselves become pure. Since our body is not our self, cleaning our body alone is not enough; we need to clean our self through purification practice.

What is it that we need to purify? We need to purify our non-virtuous and inappropriate actions. In our countless previous lives we performed many actions that caused other living beings to experience suffering and problems and, as a result of these non-virtuous actions, we now experience many different problems and sufferings. Although the actions themselves have ceased, their potential to give rise to suffering and problems still remains on our subtle consciousness, and will remain for life after life until it ripens. Therefore, on our root consciousness there are infinite negative potentials, which function to lead us into wrong paths and to experience endless suffering. These are serious obstacles to our Dharma practice in general, and to our practice of Mahamudra Tantra in particular.

We can understand how our non-virtuous potentials are the main obstacle to our Dharma practice through contemplating the following:

In our previous lives we performed actions that rejected holy Dharma, and denied rebirth, karma and the attainment of liberation and enlightenment. As a result of this we now experience (1) difficulties in developing the intention to practise Dharma, (2) difficulties in believing Dharma teachings, such as karma, and (3) difficulties in making progress in our Dharma practice.

Purification practice is very simple. All we need to do is contemplate the great disadvantages of the non-virtuous

Panchen Losang Yeshe

actions that we have performed since beginningless time. Then, with strong regret we confess all these non-virtuous actions, as well as transgressions of our vows and commitments, to Lama Losang Buddha Heruka, and to all the other holy beings, while reciting the following verse:

Whatever non-virtues of body, speech, and mind
I have accumulated since time without beginning,
Especially transgressions of my three vows,
With great remorse I confess each one from the depths of
   my heart.

We should repeat this practice many times. At the end of each session we make a strong determination not to perform any non-virtuous action or to transgress any of our vows and commitments. As the great preliminary guide for our Mahamudra practice, we can collect a hundred thousand recitations of this verse – concentrating strongly on its meaning. Alternatively we can collect a hundred thousand recitations of Vajrasattva's mantra.

REJOICING

We should learn to rejoice in others' virtuous actions, happiness, good qualities and good fortune. Normally we do the opposite and develop jealousy. Jealousy is very harmful for individuals and society. In an instant it can destroy our own and others' happiness and harmony, and lead to fighting, or even war. In everyday life we can see how people react with jealousy in regard to relationships, business, position and religious views, causing suffering to so many people. Our problems of jealousy can be solved simply by learning to rejoice in others' happiness and goodness. This can be practised even while we are lying down, relaxing, or going about our daily activities.

With very little effort we can accumulate immeasurable good fortune simply by rejoicing in the excellent deeds of Buddhas such as Je Tsongkhapa. We can do this while reciting the following verse with strong concentration on the meaning:

In this degenerate age you strove for much learning and
*   accomplishment.*
Abandoning the eight worldly concerns, you made your
*   freedom and endowment meaningful.*
O Protector, from the very depths of my heart,
I rejoice in the great wave of your deeds.

REQUESTING THE TURNING OF THE WHEEL OF DHARMA

We begin this practice by thinking:

I have the opportunity to listen to, understand and practise
holy Dharma, and therefore the good fortune to enter, make
progress along and complete the path to enlightenment.
How wonderful it would be if all other living beings could
enjoy the same good fortune!

From the depths of our heart we then repeatedly request Lama Losang Buddha Heruka to emanate countless Spiritual Teachers to teach holy Dharma and guide all living beings to the state of ultimate happiness, enlightenment, while reciting the following verse:

From the billowing clouds of wisdom and compassion
In the space of your Truth Body, O Venerable and holy
*   Gurus,*
Please send down a rain of vast and profound Dharma
Appropriate to the disciples of this world.

DEDICATION

Whenever we perform any virtuous actions, we should dedicate them to the attainment of enlightenment and to the flourishing of Buddha's doctrine, which benefits all living beings. The great Master Atisha said:

Dedicate your virtues throughout the day and the night, and always watch your mind.

By dedicating our virtuous actions in this way, their potentialities will never be destroyed by anger and wrong views but instead will increase in strength. The practice of dedication makes our virtuous actions effective. We can engage in this practice while reciting the following verse:

Through the virtues I have accumulated here,
May the doctrine and all living beings receive every benefit.
Especially may the essence of the doctrine
Of Venerable Losang Dragpa shine forever.

MANDALA OFFERING

Another special offering is the mandala offering. The word 'mandala' in this context refers to the entire universe, which can be divided into four lands, or continents: the eastern, southern, western and northern continents. For enlightened beings this universe is a Pure Land because their minds are completely pure and they have no impure experience or perceptions. Thus, with the intention to liberate all living beings from their suffering permanently, we offer this entire universe as a Pure Land to Lama Losang Buddha Heruka, and to all the other holy beings, while reciting the following words:

The ground sprinkled with perfume and spread with
  flowers,
The Great Mountain, four lands, sun and moon,
Seen as a Buddha Land and offered thus,
May all beings enjoy such Pure Lands.

IDAM GURU RATNA MANDALAKAM NIRYATAYAMI

We should offer a mandala every day, at any time. As the great preliminary guide for our Mahamudra practice we should collect a hundred thousand mandala offerings, either throughout our daily life or in retreat. Detailed explanations can be found in *Guide to Dakini Land* and *Great Treasury of Merit*.

REQUESTING ATTAINMENTS OF THE STAGES OF THE PATH

Having offered the seven limbs and the mandala, from the depths of our heart we then make requests to the holy beings in the space before us to bestow upon us the attainments of the stages of the path to enlightenment. We do this while reciting the following prayers, concentrating strongly on their meaning:

The *Migtsema* prayer

Tsongkhapa, crown ornament of the scholars of the Land
    of the Snows,
You are Avalokiteshvara, the treasury of unobservable
    compassion,
Manjushri, the supreme stainless wisdom,
And Vajrapani, the destroyer of the hosts of maras;
O Losang Dragpa I request you, please grant your
    blessings.   (3x, 7x, 21x or more)

Prayer of the Stages of the Path

The path begins with strong reliance
On my kind Teacher, source of all good;
O Bless me with this understanding
To follow him with great devotion.

This human life with all its freedoms,
Extremely rare, with so much meaning;
O Bless me with this understanding
All day and night to seize its essence.

My body, like a water bubble,
Decays and dies so very quickly;
After death come results of karma,
Just like the shadow of a body.

With this firm knowledge and remembrance
Bless me to be extremely cautious,
Always avoiding harmful actions
And gathering abundant virtue.

Samsara's pleasures are deceptive,
Give no contentment, only torment;
So please bless me to strive sincerely
To gain the bliss of perfect freedom.

O Bless me so that from this pure thought
Come mindfulness and greatest caution,
To keep as my essential practice
The doctrine's root, the Pratimoksha.

Just like myself all my kind mothers
Are drowning in samsara's ocean;
O So that I may soon release them,
Bless me to train in bodhichitta.

But I cannot become a Buddha
By this alone without three ethics;
So bless me with the strength to practise
The Bodhisattva's ordination.

By pacifying my distractions
And analyzing perfect meanings,
Bless me to quickly gain the union
Of special insight and quiescence.

When I become a pure container
Through common paths, bless me to enter
The essence practice of good fortune,
The supreme vehicle, Vajrayana.

The two attainments both depend on
My sacred vows and my commitments;
Bless me to understand this clearly
And keep them at the cost of my life.

By constant practice in four sessions,
The way explained by holy Teachers,
O Bless me to gain both the stages,
Which are the essence of the Tantras.

May those who guide me on the good path,
And my companions all have long lives;
Bless me to pacify completely
All obstacles, outer and inner.

May I always find perfect Teachers,
And take delight in holy Dharma,
Accomplish all grounds and paths swiftly,
And gain the state of Vajradhara.

All the above, from going for refuge to the *Prayer of the Stages of the Path*, can be practised in one session in conjunction with the prayer *Heart Jewel*, which can be found in Appendix V.

As the great preliminary guide of Guru yoga for our Mahamudra practice, we can collect a hundred thousand recitations of the name mantra of Lama Losang Buddha Heruka. The practice of this mantra is the very essence of Guru yoga, and we should practise it with strong faith and devotion. The mantra is:

OM GURU SUMATI BUDDHA HERUKA SARWA SIDDHI HUM

When we recite 'OM GURU SUMATI BUDDHA HERUKA' we are calling Lama Losang Buddha Heruka, and with 'SARWA SIDDHI HUM' we are requesting him to bestow all the attainments of the stages of the path – from the realization of relying upon our Spiritual Guide up to the state of Vajradhara, Buddhahood.

From time to time we should also recite the following *Seven-line Prayer of Request to Heruka*, while concentrating on the meaning:

O Guru Heruka, synthesis of all Three Jewels,
Please bestow your blessings upon myself and all living
*   beings;*
Please release my mind from inappropriate attention and
*   mistaken conceptions,*
And transform it into the profound path that leads to the
*   union of outer and inner Dakini Land;*
Please free me from all outer and inner obstacles.
I have no refuge other than you,
So please, please care for me with your great compassion.

RECEIVING BLESSINGS

After making these requests, we imagine that all the other holy beings around Je Tsongkhapa dissolve into him. Je Tsongkhapa then dissolves into Buddha Shakyamuni, who dissolves into Heruka. With delight, Heruka comes to our crown, where he diminishes to the size of a thumb. He then enters through the crown of our head and comes to the centre of our crown channel wheel, where he blesses our central channel at the level of our crown. Then he descends through our central channel, reaches the centre of our throat channel wheel and blesses our central channel at the level of our throat. Again, he descends through our central channel, reaches the centre of our heart channel wheel and blesses our central channel at the level of our heart as well as our indestructible wind and mind. Finally, Heruka dissolves into our indestructible mind at our heart. We strongly believe that our indestructible mind receives a special power that transforms it into the union of great bliss and emptiness. We meditate on this feeling single-pointedly without distraction.

This special way of receiving blessings is practised in conjunction with the following three verses:

O Glorious and precious root Guru,
Please sit on the lotus and moon seat at my heart.
Please care for me with your great kindness,
And grant me the blessings of your body, speech, and mind.

O Glorious and precious root Guru,
Please sit on the lotus and moon seat at my heart.
Please care for me with your great kindness,
And bestow the common and supreme attainments.

O Glorious and precious root Guru,
Please sit on the lotus and moon seat at my heart.
Please care for me with your great kindness,
And remain firm until I attain the essence of enlightenment.

There are now two ways of training in Mahamudra: (1) training in meditation on the central channel, the indestructible drop, and the indestructible wind and mind, and (2) the six stages of training in Mahamudra. I have already explained how to meditate on the central channel, indestructible drop, and indestructible wind and mind. I will now explain the six stages of training in Mahamudra.

Losang Trinlay

The Six Stages of Training in Mahamudra

This way of training in Mahamudra is very special. Its temporary purpose is to make our mind progressively more subtle and therefore more peaceful; and to reduce our delusions such as anger and attachment so that we can solve many of our daily problems. However, the ultimate aim of this training is eventually to realize directly our continuously residing mind and thus attain enlightenment quickly. The six stages are:

1 Identifying our own mind
2 Realizing our mind directly
3 Identifying our subtle mind
4 Realizing our subtle mind directly
5 Identifying our very subtle mind
6 Realizing our very subtle mind directly

In the Sutras and Mahamudra scriptures it says:

If you realize your own mind you will become a Buddha; you should not seek Buddhahood elsewhere.

According to Highest Yoga Tantra, the meaning of these words is that if we realize our continuously residing mind directly we become a Buddha; we do not need to seek Buddhahood elsewhere.

Suppose there is a person who wants to see a particular city by taking a train journey that passes through six stations. First it is important that he or she gets to the first station, then he must pass through each of the other stations until he reaches the sixth station, from where he will be able to see that city directly. In a similar way, we want to see the city of enlightenment by journeying on the 'train' of training in Mahamudra, which has six stages. First, it is important that we reach the first stage, identifying our own mind, and then we must pass through the remaining stages until we reach the sixth stage – realizing our own very subtle mind directly – from where we can see the city of enlightenment directly.

IDENTIFYING OUR OWN MIND

We have identified our own mind when we understand clearly its location, nature and function.

Generally it looks as if we know our mind. We all have minds and we all know what state our mind is in – whether it is happy or sad, clear or confused, positive or negative, and so on. However, if someone were to ask us what the nature of our mind is, how it functions and where it is located, we would probably not be able to give a precise answer. This indicates that we do not have a clear understanding of the mind.

Because of not knowing our own mind, we identify it incorrectly. Most people when asked what the mind is will probably point to their heads and say that it is the brain, but this is incorrect. Our mind is principally located in the region of our heart channel wheel, or heart chakra. Its nature is clarity. This means that it is empty, like clear space, and that it is a formless continuum completely lacking shape and colour, which possesses the actual power to perceive, understand and remember objects.

It is not easy to understand precisely the meaning of 'clarity' in this context. Put simply, clarity means something that is clear enough to perceive objects. Although, for example, clear glass, a clear sky or a clean mirror are clear, they are not clear enough to perceive objects. They cannot perceive objects because they are inanimate objects, and although we can see reflections in a mirror, for example, the mirror itself cannot perceive objects. Although we say 'I perceive objects', we do so only through the power of mind. A person or self is not clarity because it is not clear enough to perceive, or cognize, objects. Only mind has the power to cognize objects; without a mind we are not able to perceive anything. Since only mind has the power to perceive objects, only clarity can be mind and only mind can be clarity.

In *Commentary to Valid Cognition* the Buddhist scholar Dharmakirti, famous for his powers of logic and reasoning, explained and clarified the most difficult aspects of Buddha's teachings. In this he defined mind as 'that which is clarity and cognizes'. This definition is completely reliable and non-deceptive. In this context, clarity is necessarily mind.

The function of the mind is to perceive or cognize objects, to understand or to impute objects. When we say that we understand something, we do so only because our mind understands it. Understanding is a function only of the mind.

Without our mind we are powerless to do anything. We are able to perform actions only through the power of our mind. We may say 'I created this' or 'I built this' or 'I painted this' and so forth, but without the mind we cannot do anything, whether ordinary or spiritual. Our speech and all our physical actions, as well as our study, contemplation and meditation, entirely depend upon our mind. Just as a computer functions only if it has electricity, without mind our body is useless. Without electricity a computer is fit only to be thrown away, and similarly without mind our body is fit only for the graveyard.

The mind has an enormous number of functions. Beauty and ugliness, good and bad, happiness and suffering – all depend upon mind. Everything we see, hear, smell, taste or touch with our sense awarenesses, or perceive with our mental awareness, is created by mind. How? Through imputation. An object only exists because the mind imputes it.

For example, a car is merely imputed by mind. Before the imputation 'car' there is no car. There may be an assembly of things that is a suitable basis upon which to impute car, but each one of these things is not the car and the assembly itself is not the car. It is only through the process of imputation that 'car' develops; the mind imputes 'car', thinking 'this is a car', and then we verbally assign the name 'car'. This is true of everything. The world, enjoyments, houses, cars, bodies, speech and we ourself all develop only through being imputed by mind.

To understand this point we can take the example of a committee choosing a chairperson to represent them. Before the election, someone is just an ordinary member of the committee but after being elected people will call him or her the Chairperson. 'Chairperson' is imputed or created by mind. First the mind thinks 'He is the Chairperson', and then verbally people say 'He is the Chairperson'. In this way, 'Chairperson' develops or is newly created through a process of imputation of mind. Ordained Sangha, for example, are monks or nuns through imputation, and we exist as Mary or John and so forth through imputation.

This is true of everything; the entire universe exists through imputation. There is not a single phenomenon that is not imputed by mind; everything depends upon imputation by mind for its existence. If we think deeply about this, we can understand that both samsara and the liberation of nirvana are created by mind, and also that we can abandon samsara and attain liberation and enlightenment simply by changing our mind.

Drubwang Losang Namgyal

Mind is therefore the creator of all things, including the entire world. In *Guide to the Middle Way* the Buddhist scholar Chandrakirti established that Buddha rejected any creator other than mind, presenting many valid reasons based on Buddha's teachings for proving that only mind is the creator of all things. As an example, we can look at the simple activity of making something, such as a table. The original idea for making something arises in our mind, and knowing how to do this also comes from our mind. We then make the design and gradually physically make the object, but every stage of this depends upon our mind. The mind is the creator and the body is like a machine that the mind uses to create and produce things. If our mind did not know how to make something, we would never be able to make it. Everything we do depends on knowing and understanding, which are functions only of mind.

Understanding that everything is created by mind helps us to understand the power of mind. Every living being is under the control of mind. In life after life, since beginningless time, we have been under its control; whatever our mind has wanted to do, without choice, like servants, we have done it. If our mind tells us to, we will kill ourself; if it says 'Kill your parents' or 'Kill your children', then without choice we are forced to do it. We created all our past bad actions because we were under the control of our mind and, unless we achieve a direct realization of emptiness in this life, we shall remain under its control, without any freedom, in countless future lives.

There is nothing more powerful than the mind. When our mind is under the control of delusions it can instantly throw us into the fires of the deepest hell. Through the kindness of Buddha's teachings, or Dharma, we now have the opportunity to understand and recognize the enemy of our delusions, and to reduce and eventually eliminate them. Dharma is the only method by which we can fully control our mind. If we fail to control our deluded mind through Dharma practice, we shall have to remain under its control and continue to experience immense suffering.

This concludes a general introduction to the mind.

To identify our own mind, the first of the six stages of training in Mahamudra, we now principally focus on four steps: seeking, finding, holding and remaining.

The first step is to seek our mind – the object of our meditation – by contemplating its location, nature, function and power, as explained above. We should memorize the essence of these instructions on the mind and contemplate their meaning again and again. In this way we try to perceive a rough mental or generic image of our mind. Initially it will seem distant and unclear but we should still feel that we are definitely focused on our mind. Gradually, as our practice progresses, it will become clearer and less distant.

When we perceive clearly a rough generic image of our mind, we have found our mind. This completes the second step, finding the object of meditation.

We then train in holding this object in meditation without forgetting. Through continually practising in this way, when we are able to hold our mind without forgetting for about one minute we accomplish the third step, holding.

Through continually practising the steps of seeking, finding and holding, we try to remain on our mind single-pointedly without forgetting, first for one minute, then two minutes, then five minutes. When we are able to do this single-pointedly for five minutes, we accomplish the fourth step, remaining. At this point, we accomplish identifying our own mind – the first stage of training in Mahamudra.

In this context, our own mind means our root mind, or root mental consciousness, mainly located at our heart. Identifying our own mind therefore means identifying our root mind. As explained in *Understanding the Mind*, there are many different types of mind, such as the fifty-one mental factors, but these are just parts or branches of mind, which are temporary and not stable. They manifest for a few minutes and then cease, manifest again later for a few minutes and then cease again. The root mind can be likened to an ocean from which all the different types of minds, as well as all appearances, arise like waves.

REALIZING OUR MIND DIRECTLY

When we attain the concentration of tranquil abiding observing our mind, we shall realize our own mind directly because this concentration is extremely clear and free from conceptual thoughts.

Tranquil abiding observing our mind is a very profound concentration. It is attained by completing nine levels of concentration called the 'nine mental abidings' observing our mind. The first and second mental abidings are called 'placing the mind' and 'continual placement'. We accomplish these first two mental abidings on the first stage – identifying our own mind – when we complete the steps of holding the object for about one minute and then remaining on it for about five minutes. Now we need to progress from the second mental abiding to the third mental abiding and so forth, until we attain the ninth mental abiding, from which we will be able to attain actual tranquil abiding observing our mind.

We progress from the second mental abiding to the third mental abiding by repeating the practice of seeking, finding, holding and remaining, exactly as described in the first stage of training in Mahamudra. Through continually training in these four steps, the duration of remaining will progressively increase from five minutes to ten minutes, then twenty minutes, one hour, and longer. During this stage, if we lose the object of meditation – the clear appearance of our own mind – we need to regain it by repeating the practice of seeking, finding, holding and remaining.

Gradually, through training in this way we are able immediately to recall the object of our meditation, whenever we lose it, by immediately remembering the nature and function of our mind without needing to repeat the steps of seeking and so forth. At this stage, we progress from the second to the third mental abiding, and our concentration of the second mental abiding – continual placement – transforms into the concentration of the third mental abiding, called 'replacement'.

How do we progress from the third to the fourth mental abiding? We continue to meditate on the concentration of the third mental abiding until we gain the ability to maintain pure concentration throughout the entire meditation session, without ever losing our object of meditation – the clear appearance of our own mind. At this stage we progress from the third to the fourth mental abiding, and our concentration of the third mental abiding transforms into the concentration of the fourth mental abiding called 'close placement'.

As mentioned above, we realize our own mind directly when we attain the concentration of tranquil abiding observing our mind. However, already through the power of the concentration of close placement we are able to control our distractions and delusions. Our understanding of our own mind, therefore, is now very clear and the power of our mindfulness and alertness is very strong. Thus, even by just attaining the concentration of the fourth mental abiding we can now engage in the third stage of training in Mahamudra – identifying our own subtle mind.

Detailed explanations of how to attain tranquil abiding can be found in *Joyful Path of Good Fortune* and *Meaningful to Behold*.

IDENTIFYING OUR SUBTLE MIND

Generally, all our waking minds are gross minds because they are mounted upon gross inner winds that flow through our left and right channels. Subtle and very subtle minds usually manifest only during deep sleep or during the death process. They are mounted upon subtle and very

Kachen Yeshe Gyaltsän

subtle inner winds, which flow through our central channel. Ordinary beings cannot identify their subtle and very subtle minds because their memory is unable to function during sleep and death. Only Highest Yoga Tantric practitioners, through the power of their meditation, can identify their subtle and very subtle minds during waking, sleep and the death process.

Meditation on the central channel, the indestructible drop, and the indestructible wind and mind is the method to manifest and realize directly our subtle and very subtle minds during waking. Although the first three stages of the six-staged training in Mahamudra are also practised with the waking mind, they are preparations for success in the next three stages of training in Mahamudra. Thus the six-staged training is the method to manifest and realize directly our subtle and very subtle minds during sleep.

In the third stage – identifying our own subtle mind – we need to meditate on our subtle mind. The nature of our subtle mind is the cessation of all gross minds, and its function is to perceive an empty like space. Since it is impossible for the subtle mind to manifest without the gross minds first ceasing, we therefore meditate on our own subtle mind as follows.

First, we stop paying attention to any object; we should not think about anything but remain like a stone or a piece of wood, without experiencing or perceiving anything. We remain in this state for a few minutes, and then we imagine that all our gross minds dissolve into our subtle mind like water bubbles disappearing into the water from which they arose. We then try to perceive our subtle mind by contemplating:

*Its nature is the cessation of all gross minds, and its function
is to perceive an empty like space.*

This is the practice of seeking. When, through contemplating in this way, we perceive clearly the generic image of our subtle mind, we have found the object of our meditation – the clear appearance of our subtle mind. This is finding. Having found our object of meditation we then need to train in holding it without forgetting until we can do so for about one minute. This is holding. When, by continually repeating the steps of seeking, finding and holding, our concentration is able to remain on its object – the clear appearance of our subtle mind – for five minutes, we accomplish the fourth step, remaining. At this point we accomplish the third stage – identifying our own subtle mind.

REALIZING OUR SUBTLE MIND DIRECTLY

In general, three things happen during deep sleep: (1) our inner winds naturally gather and dissolve within the central channel, (2) all our gross minds dissolve, and (3) our subtle and very subtle minds manifest. For ordinary beings, the duration of these three is very short because they quickly pass through to dreaming or waking. However, when we accomplish the first three stages of the six-staged training in Mahamudra we are able to control our distractions, our mindfulness and alertness are very powerful and we have great familiarity with meditation on our own subtle mind, while experiencing the cessation of gross minds. Because of this, even during deep sleep, we can maintain mindfulness of our own subtle mind and prevent distractions of both our dream and waking minds from arising, so the duration of our deep sleep will be very long.

During a long deep sleep we can meditate on our own subtle mind and, when our inner winds naturally gather and dissolve within our central channel, we can recognize the signs of dissolution. When, through training in this way, we gain a clear and deep realization of our subtle minds of the white appearance, red increase and black near-attainment of sleep, we accomplish the fourth stage of training in Mahamudra – realizing our own subtle mind directly.

IDENTIFYING OUR VERY SUBTLE MIND

Having accomplished the fourth stage of training in Mahamudra, we continue to meditate on our own subtle mind during long deep sleep, and when our inner winds naturally gather and dissolve within our central channel we are able to recognize the signs of dissolution from the mirage-like appearance to the clear light. The mind of clear light is our very subtle mind.

When our very subtle clear light mind of sleep manifests we should realize that its nature is a bliss arisen from the melting of drops inside our central channel, its function is to perceive an empty like space, and its location is the very centre of our heart channel wheel. Through realizing our very subtle mind in this way, when the clear appearance of our very subtle mind of sleep becomes stable we accomplish the fifth stage of training in Mahamudra – identifying our own very subtle mind.

REALIZING OUR VERY SUBTLE MIND DIRECTLY

Having accomplished the fifth stage of training in Mahamudra, whenever we sleep we should practise two things: (1) prevent dreaming and waking from occuring, through the force of our subtle mindfulness and alertness, so that our sleep will be deep and of long duration, and (2) whenever our mind of the clear light of sleep, whose nature is bliss, manifests it meditates on the emptiness of all phenomena. We need to repeat this practice again and again.

When, by doing this meditation continually, our mind of clear light of bliss realizes emptiness directly we accomplish the sixth stage of training in Mahamudra – realizing our own very subtle mind directly. At the same time, our mind of clear light of bliss transforms into the union of great bliss and emptiness, the actual Mahamudra. Subsequently, we shall attain the union of pure illusory body and meaning clear light, from which we can see the city of enlightenment – the enlightened world.

From the point of view of accomplishing these attainments using sleep, our sleep has so much meaning! These instructions on the six stages of training in Mahamudra are very blessed instructions. Through sincerely putting these instructions into practice, many of Je Tsongkhapa's disciples, including ordained Sangha, attained full enlightenment very quickly, within three years and three months.

PART THREE

What is Emptiness?

Phurchog Ngawang Jampa

What is Emptiness?

As mentioned above, Mahamudra Tantra is defined as a mind of fully qualified clear light that experiences great bliss and realizes emptiness directly. What is emptiness? Emptiness is not nothingness, but is the real nature of phenomena. Since it is a very profound subject you will need to read the following explanation carefully, with a positive mind, and think about it deeply. It may seem very technical at first but please be patient and do not waste this precious opportunity to understand such a meaningful subject. Until we abandon our self-grasping ignorance, we shall have no real happiness because self-grasping destroys our inner peace, or mental peace. The only direct method for eliminating this ignorance is the realization of emptiness.

Ultimate truth, emptiness and ultimate nature of phenomena are the same. We should know that all our problems arise because we do not realize ultimate truth. The reason we remain in samsara's prison is that due to our delusions we continue to engage in contaminated actions.

All our delusions stem from self-grasping ignorance. Self-grasping ignorance is the source of all our negativity and problems, and the only way to eradicate it is to realize emptiness. Emptiness is not easy to understand, but it is extremely important that we make the effort. Ultimately our efforts will be rewarded by the permanent cessation of all suffering and the everlasting bliss of full enlightenment.

THE PURPOSE OF MEDITATING ON EMPTINESS

The purpose of understanding and meditating on emptiness is to release our mind from wrong conceptions and mistaken appearances so that we shall become a completely pure, or enlightened, being. In this context, 'wrong conception' refers to the mind of self-grasping ignorance – a conceptual mind that grasps objects as truly existent; and 'mistaken appearance' refers to the appearance of truly existent objects. The former are the obstructions to liberation and the latter the obstructions to omniscience. Only a Buddha has abandoned both obstructions.

First we should recognize our self-grasping, which always abides at our heart destroying our inner peace. Its nature is a wrong awareness that mistakenly believes ourself and others to be truly, or inherently, existent. This is an ignorant mind because in reality things do not exist inherently – they exist as mere imputations. Because the foolish mind of self-grasping believes or grasps at 'I', 'mine' and all other phenomena as truly existent, we develop attachment to those things we like and hatred for those we do not like. We then perform various actions that harm other living beings and, as a result, we experience various sufferings and problems throughout this life and in life after life; this is the fundamental reason why we experience so many problems. Because our sense of truly existent 'I' and 'mine' is so strong, our self-grasping also acts as the basis of all our daily problems.

Self-grasping can be likened to a poisonous tree, other delusions to its branches, and all our sufferings to its fruits; it is the fundamental source of all other delusions and all our sufferings and problems. Understanding this, we should apply great effort to recognize, reduce and finally abandon this ignorance completely.

It is not easy to recognize our ignorance of self-grasping because it is very subtle. On the one hand we know that our self-grasping – our sense of 'I' and 'mine' – is very strong; but on the other hand if we try to recognize our self-grasping it becomes very subtle! It is very rare to find a person who recognizes his or her own self-grasping unmistakenly. This is because generally people lack the understanding of the real nature of persons and phenomena, that is, their emptiness.

Without recognizing our delusion of self-grasping ignorance, we cannot reduce its power and thus we have no ability to control our delusions. If we have no ability to control our delusions, we have no method to solve our human problems. We may think that modern technology is the method to solve human problems, but if this were so then necessarily the more technology improves the fewer problems human beings would experience. However, we know this is not true; technology itself causes many new problems to arise.

There are two types of self-grasping: self-grasping of persons and self-grasping of phenomena. The first grasps our own or others' self, or I, as truly existent, and the second grasps any phenomenon other than our own or others' self as truly existent. Minds that grasp our body, our mind, our possessions and our world as truly existent are all examples of self-grasping of phenomena.

The main point of meditating on emptiness is to reduce and finally to eliminate both types of self-grasping. Self-grasping is the source of all our problems; the extent to which we suffer is directly proportional to the intensity of our self-grasping. For example, when our self-grasping is very strong we feel a sharp mental pain when others simply tease us in a friendly way, whereas at times when our self-grasping is weak we just laugh with them. Once we completely destroy our self-grasping, all our problems will naturally disappear. Even temporarily, meditating on emptiness is very helpful for overcoming anxiety and worry.

If during the meditation session we come to a clear understanding and firm realization that all phenomena lack inherent existence, this will strongly influence our mind during the meditation break. Even though the things we see around us appear to exist inherently, we shall immediately remember from our own experience during meditation that they do not exist in that way. We shall be like a magician who immediately realizes that his magical creations are just illusions.

We can check to see if our meditation on emptiness is working by observing whether or not our self-grasping is becoming weaker. If after studying, contemplating and meditating for several months or even years our self-grasping is just as strong as it was before, we can be sure that our understanding or our meditation is faulty. We have suffered from self-grasping since beginningless time and we cannot expect to eliminate it overnight, but if we meditate on emptiness regularly we should notice a gradual reduction in its strength. If by contemplating emptiness we are able to subdue our delusions – for example, overcoming our anger by reflecting how the object of our anger does not exist from its own side, or reducing the intensity of our attachment by realizing that the object of our attachment is not inherently desirable – this is proof that our understanding of emptiness is correct.

The extent to which we are able to solve our inner problems by meditating on the true nature of things depends upon two factors: the accuracy of our understanding, and our familiarity with this knowledge. Therefore, first we need to study emptiness in order to gain an intellectual understanding, and then we need to meditate on this understanding over and over again in order to deepen our familiarity.

When our body is sick we immediately try to find a cure, but there are no hospitals or medicines that can cure the mental sickness of our delusions. We consider a disease such as cancer to be a terrible thing, but in reality cancer is not so bad. Cancer is just a temporary sickness that will end the moment this present body disintegrates at death. Far

121

Panchen Palden Yeshe

worse than any physical illness is the internal sickness of our delusions, for there is no end to the suffering this can cause us. Because of our attachment to the fulfilment of our own wishes we experience continual mental pain, life after life. It can lead to conflict, murder and even suicide, and it forces us to act in ways that lead to immense suffering in future lives. Similarly, anger, jealousy and other delusions continually cause us harm. It does not matter whether we are healthy or unhealthy, rich or poor, successful or unsuccessful, popular or unpopular, we are never free from the threat of delusions. We might be quietly reading a book when suddenly, for no apparent reason, we remember an insult or an object of attachment and become unhappy. It is rare to enjoy even one hour of mental peace undisturbed by delusions.

We have endured the internal sickness of delusions since beginningless time. We brought it with us from our previous lives, suffer from it throughout this life, and will take it with us into our future lives. Doctors cannot cure it, and it will never end by itself. The only medicine with the power to cure our inner sickness is the medicine of Buddha's teachings, and especially the teachings on emptiness. All Buddha's teachings are methods to cure our inner sickness. For example, by putting Buddha's teachings on love and patience into practice we shall gain some respite from the sickness of anger, and by putting his teachings on impermanence and the disadvantages of samsara into practice we shall find some relief from the sickness of attachment. However, the only way that we can ever completely cure all our mental sicknesses is by gaining a direct realization of emptiness.

Once we realize emptiness directly, we have complete freedom. We can even control our death and choose our rebirth. Right now we may be making plans for our next holiday or our retirement, but we cannot be sure that we shall be alive even for our next meal. After we die there is no certainty where we shall be reborn; just because we are human now is no guarantee that in our next life we shall not take rebirth as an animal. Even if we are reborn human, there is no real happiness. We are born amidst blood and screams, and are completely unable to comprehend anything that is happening to us. The possessions, knowledge and friends that we worked so hard to accumulate in our previous life are all lost, and we come into the world empty-handed, confused and alone. As we grow older we have to experience all the sufferings of human life, such as ageing, sickness, hunger, thirst, fighting, having to part with what we like, having to encounter what we do not like, and failing to satisfy our desires. This does not happen in just this one life, but in life after life, over and over again. If we had to experience this suffering for just one or several lives, perhaps we could just accept it; but this suffering will be repeated over and over again, without end. How can we bear this?

We should contemplate these points until we reach a definite conclusion:

I cannot tolerate this meaningless cycle of suffering a moment longer. I must escape from samsara. Before I die, I must attain a deep experience of emptiness.

We then turn our attention to other living beings by thinking:

To remain in the prison of samsara myself is unbearable, yet all other living beings are in exactly the same situation. Moreover, when I suffer only one person suffers, whereas when others suffer countless living beings suffer. How can I bear the thought of countless living beings experiencing suffering without end? I must liberate them all from suffering. To free all living beings from suffering I must become a Buddha, and to become a Buddha I must realize ultimate truth, emptiness.

When we study emptiness it is important to do so with the right motivation. There is little benefit in studying emptiness if we just approach it as an intellectual exercise. Emptiness is difficult enough to understand, but if we approach it with an incorrect motivation this will obscure the meaning even further. However, if we study with a good motivation, faith in Buddha's teachings, and the understanding that a knowledge of emptiness can solve all our problems and enable us to help everyone else solve theirs, we shall receive Buddha's wisdom blessings and understand emptiness with greater ease. Even if we cannot understand all the technical reasoning, we shall get a feeling for emptiness, and we shall be able to subdue our delusions and solve our daily problems through contemplation and meditation on emptiness. Gradually our wisdom will increase until it transforms into the wisdom of superior seeing and finally into a direct realization of emptiness.

As our merit increases through our increased good heart and pure motivation, our meditation on emptiness will become more effective, until eventually it becomes so powerful that we destroy our self-grasping. There is no greater method for experiencing peace of mind and happiness than to meditate on emptiness. Since it is self-grasping that keeps us bound to samsara and is the source of all our suffering, meditation on emptiness is the universal solution to all problems. It is the medicine that cures all mental and physical diseases, and the nectar that bestows the everlasting happiness of enlightenment.

Emptiness is the way things really are. It is the way things exist as opposed to the way they appear. We naturally believe that the things we see around us, such as tables, chairs and houses are truly existent, because we believe that they exist in exactly the way that they appear. However, the way things appear to our senses is deceptive and completely contradictory to the way in which they actually exist. Things appear to exist from their own side, without depending upon our mind. This book that appears to our mind, for example, seems to have its own independent, objective existence. It seems to be 'outside' whereas our mind seems to be 'inside'. We feel that the book can exist without our mind; we do not feel that our mind is in any way involved in bringing the book into existence. This way of existing independent of our mind is variously called 'true existence', 'inherent existence', 'existence from its own side' and 'existence from the side of the object'.

Although things appear directly to our senses to be truly, or inherently, existent, in reality all phenomena lack, or are empty of, true existence. This book, our body, our friends, we ourself, and the entire universe are in reality just appearances to mind, like things seen in a dream. If we dream of an elephant, the elephant appears vividly in all its detail – we can see it, hear it, smell it and touch it – but when we wake up we realize that it was just an appearance to mind. We do not wonder 'Where is the elephant now?', because we understand that it was simply a projection of our mind and had no existence outside our mind. When the dream awareness that apprehended the elephant ceased, the elephant did not go anywhere – it simply disappeared, for it was just an appearance to the mind and did not exist separately from the mind. Buddha said that the same is true for all phenomena; they are mere appearances to mind, totally dependent upon the minds that perceive them.

The world we experience when we are awake and the world we experience when we are dreaming are very similar, for both are mere appearances to mind that arise from our karma. If we want to say that the dream world is false we also have to say that the waking world is false, and if we want to say that the waking world is true we also have to say that the dream world is true. The only difference between them is that the dream world is an appearance to our subtle dreaming mind whereas the waking world is an appearance to our gross waking mind. The dream world exists only for as long as the dream awareness to which it appears exists, and the waking world exists only for as long as the waking awareness to which it appears exists. When we die, our gross waking minds dissolve into our very subtle mind and the world we experienced when we were alive simply disappears. The world as others perceive it will continue, but our personal world will disappear as completely and irrevocably as the world of last night's dream.

Khädrub Ngawang Dorje

Buddha said that all phenomena are like illusions. There are many different types of illusion, such as mirages, rainbows or drug-induced hallucinations. In ancient times there used to be magicians who would cast a spell over their audience, causing them to see objects, such as a piece of wood, as something else, such as a tiger. Those deceived by the spell would see what appeared to be a real tiger and develop fear, but those who arrived after the spell had been cast would simply see a piece of wood. What all illusions have in common is that the way they appear does not coincide with the way they exist. Buddha likened all phenomena to illusions because, through the force of the imprints of self-grasping ignorance accumulated since beginningless time, whatever appears to our mind naturally appears to be truly existent and we instinctively assent to this appearance, but in reality everything is totally empty of true existence. Like a mirage that appears to be water but is not in fact water, things appear in a deceptive way. Not understanding their real nature we are fooled by appearances, and grasp at books and tables, bodies and worlds as truly existent. The result of grasping at phenomena in this way is that we develop self-cherishing, attachment, hatred, jealousy and other delusions, our mind becomes agitated and unbalanced, and our inner peace is destroyed. We are like travellers in a desert who exhaust themselves running after mirages, or like someone walking down a road at night mistaking the shadows of the trees for criminals or wild animals waiting to attack.

THE EMPTINESS OF OUR BODY

To understand how phenomena are empty of true, or inherent, existence we should consider our own body. Once we have understood how our body lacks true existence we can easily apply the same reasoning to other objects.

In *Guide to the Bodhisattva's Way of Life* Bodhisattva Shantideva says:

Therefore, there is no body,
But, because of ignorance, we perceive a body within
    the hands and so forth,
Just like a mind mistakenly apprehending a person
When observing the shape of a pile of stones at
    dusk.

On one level we know our body very well – we know whether it is healthy or unhealthy, beautiful or ugly, and so forth. However we never examine it more deeply, asking ourself: 'What precisely is my body? Where is my body? What is its real nature?' If we did examine our body in this way we would not be able to find it – instead of finding our body the result of this examination would be that our body disappears. The meaning of the first part of Shantideva's verse, 'Therefore, there is no body', is that if we search for our 'real' body, there is no body; and also there is no body within our hands and so forth. Our body exists only if we do not search for a real body behind its mere appearance.

There are two ways of searching for an object. An example of the first way, which we can call a 'conventional search', is searching for our car in a car park. The conclusion of this type of search is that we find the car, in the sense that we see the thing that everyone agrees is our car. However, having located our car in the car park, suppose we are still not satisfied with the mere appearance of the car and we want to determine exactly what is the car. We might then engage in what we can call an 'ultimate search' for the car, in which we look within the object itself to find something that is the object. To do this we ask ourself: 'Are any of the individual parts of the car, the car? Are the wheels the car? Is the engine the car? Is the chassis the car?', and so forth. When conducting an ultimate search for our car we are not satisfied with just pointing to the bonnet, wheels, and so forth and then saying 'car'; we want to know what the car really is. Instead of just using the word 'car' as ordinary people do, we want to know what the word really refers to. We want to mentally separate the car from all that is not car, so that we can say: 'This is what the car really is, this is the truly existent car.'

To understand Shantideva's claim that in reality there is no body, we need to conduct an ultimate search for our body. If we are ordinary beings, all objects, including our body, appear to exist inherently. As mentioned above, objects seem to be independent of our mind and independent of other phenomena. The universe appears to consist of discrete objects that have an existence from their own side. These objects appear to exist in themselves as stars, planets, mountains, people and so forth, 'waiting' to be experienced by conscious beings. Normally it does not occur to us that we are involved in any way in the existence of these phenomena. For example, we feel that our body exists in its own right and does not depend upon our mind, or anyone else's, to bring it into existence. However, if our body did exist in the way that we instinctively grasp it – as an external object rather than just a projection of mind – we should be able to point to our body without pointing to any phenomenon that is not our body. We should be able to find it amongst its parts or outside its parts. Since there is no third possibility, if our body cannot be found either amongst its parts or outside its parts we must conclude that our body does not exist as an objective entity.

It is not difficult to understand that the individual parts of our body are not our body – it is absurd to say that our back, our legs, or our head are our body. If one of the parts, say our back, is our body, then the other parts are equally our body, and it would follow that we have many bodies. Furthermore, our back, legs and so forth cannot be our body because they are parts of our body. The body is the part-possessor, and the back, legs and so forth are the possessed parts; and possessor and possessed cannot be one and the same.

Some people, including even followers of some schools of Buddhist philosophy, believe that although none of the individual parts of the body is the body, the collection of all the parts assembled together is the body. According to these schools it is possible to find our body when we search for it analytically because the collection of all the parts of our body is our body. However, followers of the highest school of Buddhist philosophy, the Madhyamika-Prasangika school, refute this assertion with many logical reasons. The force of these reasons may not be immediately obvious to us, but if we contemplate them carefully with a calm and positive mind we shall come to appreciate their validity.

Since none of the individual parts of our body is our body, how can the collection of all the parts be our body? For example, a collection of dogs cannot be a human being, because none of the individual dogs is human. As each individual member is 'non-human', how can this collection of non-humans magically transform into a human? Similarly, since the collection of the parts of our body is a collection of things that are not our body, it cannot be our body. Just as the collection of dogs remains simply dogs, so the collection of all the parts of our body remains simply parts of our body – it does not magically transform into the part-possessor, our body.

We may find this point difficult to understand, but if we think about it for a long time with a calm and positive mind, and discuss it with more experienced practitioners, it will gradually become clearer. We can also consult authentic books on the subject, such as *Heart of Wisdom*.

There is another way in which we can know that the collection of the parts of our body is not our body. If we can point to the collection of the parts of our body and say that this is, in itself, our body, then the collection of the parts of our body must exist independently of all phenomena that are not our body. Thus it would follow that the collection of the parts of our body exists independently of the parts themselves. This is clearly absurd – if it were true, we could remove all the parts of our body and the collection of the parts would remain. We can therefore conclude that the collection of the parts of our body is not our body.

Ngulchu Dharmabhadra

Since the body cannot be found within its parts, either as an individual part or as the collection, the only possibility that remains is that it exists separately from its parts. If this is the case, it should be possible mentally or physically to remove all the parts of our body and still be left with the body. However, if we remove our arms, our legs, our head, our trunk, and all the other parts of our body, no body is left. This proves that there is no body separate from its parts. Whenever we point to our body we are pointing only to a part of our body, which is not our body.

We have now searched in every possible place and have been unable to find our body either amongst its parts or anywhere else. We can find nothing that corresponds to the vividly appearing body that we normally grasp at. We are forced to agree with Shantideva that when we search for our body there is no body to be found. This clearly indicates that our body does not exist from its own side, independently of mind. It is almost as if our body does not exist. Indeed, the only sense in which we can say that our body does exist is if we are satisfied with the mere name 'body' and do not expect to find a real body behind the name. If we try to find, or point to, a real body to which the name 'body' refers, we shall not find anything at all. Instead of finding a truly existent body we shall perceive the non-existence, or emptiness, of such a body. We shall realize that the body we normally perceive, grasp at, and cherish does not exist at all. This non-existence of the body we normally grasp at is the true, or ultimate, nature of our body.

The term 'true nature' is very meaningful. Not being satisfied with the mere appearance and name 'body' we examined our body to discover its true nature. The result of this examination was a definite non-finding of our body. Where we expected to find a truly existent body we discovered the utter non-existence of that truly existent body. This non-existence, or emptiness, is the true nature of our body. Apart from the mere absence of a truly existent body there is no other true nature of our body – every other attribute of the body is just part of its deceptive nature. Since this is the case, why do we spend so much time focusing on the deceptive nature of our body? At present we ignore the true nature of our body and other phenomena, and concentrate only on their deceptive nature; yet the result of concentrating all the time on deceptive objects is that our mind becomes disturbed and we remain in samsara. If we wish to experience pure peace we must acquaint our mind with the truth. Instead of wasting our energy focusing only on meaningless, deceptive objects, we should focus on the true nature of things.

Although it is impossible to find our body when we search for it analytically, when we do not engage in analysis our body appears very clearly. Why is this? Shantideva says that due to ignorance we see a body within the hands and other parts of our body. It is ignorance, not wisdom, that makes us see a body within its parts. In reality there is no body within its parts. Just as at dusk we might see a pile of stones as a man even though there is no man within the stones, so in the same way our ignorance sees a body within the collection of arms, legs and so forth, even though no body exists there. The body we see within the collection of arms and legs is simply an hallucination of our ignorant mind. Not recognizing it as such, however, we grasp at it very strongly, cherish it, and exhaust ourself in trying to protect it from any discomfort.

The way to familiarize our mind with the true nature of the body is to use the above reasoning to search for our body and then, when we have searched in every possible place and not found it, to concentrate on the space-like emptiness that is the mere absence of the truly existent body. This space-like emptiness is the true nature of our body. Although it resembles empty space, it is a meaningful emptiness. Its meaning is the utter non-existence of the truly existent body that we grasp at so strongly and have cherished all our life.

Through becoming familiar with the experience of the space-like ultimate nature of the body, our grasping at our body will be reduced. As a result we shall experience far less suffering, anxiety and frustration in relation to our body. Our physical tension will diminish and our health will improve, and even when we do become sick our physical discomfort will not disturb our mind. Those who have a direct experience of emptiness do not feel any pain even if they are beaten or shot. Knowing that the real nature of their body is like space, for them being beaten is like space being beaten and being shot is like space being shot. Moreover, good and bad external conditions no longer have the power to disturb their mind, because they realize them to be like a magician's illusion, with no existence separate from the mind. Instead of being pulled about by changing conditions like a puppet on a string, their minds remain free and tranquil in the knowledge of the equal and unchanging ultimate nature of all things. In this way, a person who directly realizes the true nature of phenomena experiences peace day and night, life after life.

We need to distinguish between the conventionally existent body that does exist and the inherently existent body that does not exist; but we must take care not to be misled by the words into thinking that the conventionally existent body is anything more than a mere appearance to mind. It is perhaps less confusing simply to say that for a mind that directly sees the truth, or emptiness, there is no body. A body exists only for a mind to which a body appears.

Shantideva advises us that unless we wish to understand emptiness we should not examine conventional truths such as our body, possessions, places and friends, but instead be satisfied with their mere names, as are worldly people. Once a worldly person knows an object's name and purpose he is satisfied that he knows the object and does not investigate further. We must do the same, unless we want to meditate on emptiness. However, we should remember that if we did examine objects more closely we would not find them, for they would simply disappear, just as a mirage disappears if we try to look for it.

The same reasoning that we have used to prove the lack of true existence of our body can be applied to all other phenomena. This book, for example, seems to exist from its own side, somewhere within its parts; but when we examine the book more precisely we discover that none of the individual pages nor the collection of the pages is the book, yet without them there is no book. Instead of finding a truly existent book we are left beholding an emptiness that is the non-existence of the book we previously held to exist. Due to our ignorance the book appears to exist separately from our mind, as if our mind were inside and the book outside, but through analyzing the book we discover that this appearance is completely false. There is no book outside the mind. There is no book 'out there', within the pages. The only way the book exists is as a mere appearance to mind, a mere projection of the mind.

All phenomena exist by way of convention; nothing is inherently existent. This applies to mind, to Buddha, and even to emptiness itself. Everything is merely imputed by mind. All phenomena have parts – physical phenomena have physical parts, and non-physical phenomena have various parts, or attributes, that can be distinguished by thought. Using the same type of reasoning as above, we can realize that any phenomenon is not one of its parts, not the collection of its parts, and not separate from its parts. In this way we can realize the emptiness of all phenomena.

It is particularly helpful to meditate on the emptiness of objects that arouse in us strong delusions like attachment or anger. By analyzing correctly we shall realize that the object we desire, or the object we dislike, does not exist from its own side. Its beauty or ugliness, and even its very existence, are imputed by mind. By thinking in this way we shall discover that there is no basis for attachment or anger.

Yangchän Drubpay Dorje

THE EMPTINESS OF OUR MIND

In *Training the Mind in Seven Points*, after outlining how to engage in analytical meditation on the emptiness of inherent existence of outer phenomena such as our body, Geshe Chekhawa continues by saying that we should then analyze our own mind to understand how it lacks inherent existence.

Our mind is not an independent entity, but an ever-changing continuum that depends upon many factors, such as its previous moments, its objects, and the inner energy winds upon which our minds are mounted. Like everything else, our mind is imputed upon a collection of many factors and therefore lacks inherent existence. A primary mind, or consciousness, for example, has five parts or 'mental factors': feeling, discrimination, intention, contact and attention. Neither the individual mental factors nor the collection of these mental factors is the primary mind itself, because they are mental factors and therefore parts of the primary mind. However, there is no primary mind that is separate from these mental factors. A primary mind is merely imputed upon the mental factors that are its basis of imputation, and therefore it does not exist from its own side.

Having identified the nature of our primary mind, which is a formless continuum that perceives objects, we then search for it within its parts – feeling, discrimination, intention, contact and attention – until finally we realize its unfindability. This unfindability is its ultimate nature, or emptiness. We then think:

Everything that appears to my mind is the nature of my mind. My mind is the nature of emptiness.

In this way we feel that everything dissolves into emptiness. We perceive only the emptiness of our mind and we meditate on this emptiness. This way of meditating on the emptiness of our mind is more profound than the meditation on the emptiness of our body. Gradually our experience of emptiness will become clearer and clearer until finally we gain an undefiled wisdom that directly realizes the emptiness of our mind.

THE EMPTINESS OF OUR I

The object we grasp at most strongly is our self or I. Due to the imprints of self-grasping ignorance accumulated over time without beginning, our I appears to us as inherently existent, and our self-grasping mind automatically grasps at it in this way. Although we grasp at an inherently existent I all the time, even during sleep, it is not easy to identify how it appears to our mind. To identify it clearly we must begin by allowing it to manifest strongly by contemplating situations in which we have an exaggerated sense of I, such as when we are embarrassed, ashamed, afraid or indignant. We recall or imagine such a situation and then, without any comment or analysis, try to gain a clear mental image of how the I naturally appears at such times. We have to be patient at this stage because it may take many sessions before we gain a clear image. Eventually we shall see that the I appears to be completely solid and real, existing from its own side without depending upon the body or the mind. This vividly appearing I is the inherently existent I that we cherish so strongly. It is the I that we defend when we are criticized and that we are so proud of when we are praised.

Once we have an image of how the I appears in these extreme circumstances, we should try to identify how it appears normally, in less extreme situations. For example, we can observe the I that is presently reading this book and try to discover how it appears to our mind. Eventually we shall see that although in this case there is not such an inflated sense of I, nevertheless the I still appears to be inherently existent, existing from its own side without depending upon the body or the mind. Once we have an image of the inherently existent I, we focus on it for a while with single-pointed concentration. Then in meditation we proceed to the next stage, which is to contemplate logical reasons to prove that the inherently existent I we are grasping at does not in fact exist.

If the I exists in the way that it appears, it must exist in one of four ways: as the body, as the mind, as the collection of the body and mind, or as something separate from the body and mind; there is no other possibility. We contemplate this carefully until we become convinced that this is the case and then we proceed to examine each of the four possibilities:

1 If the I is the body, there is no sense in saying 'my body', because the possessor and the possessed are identical.

143

If the I is the body, there is no rebirth because the I ceases when the body dies.

If the I and the body are identical, then since we are capable of developing faith, dreaming, solving mathematical puzzles, and so on, it follows that flesh, blood, and bones can do the same.

Since none of this is true, it follows that the I is not the body.

2 If the I is the mind, there is no sense in saying 'my mind', because the possessor and the possessed are identical; but usually when we focus on our mind we say 'my mind'. This clearly indicates that the I is not the mind.

If the I is the mind, then since each person has many types of mind, such as the six conscious-nesses, conceptual minds, and non-conceptual minds, it follows that each person has just as many I's. Since this is absurd, the I cannot be the mind.

3 Since the body is not the I and the mind is not the I, the collection of the body and mind cannot be the I. The collection of the body and mind is a collection of things that are not the I, so how can the collection itself be the I? For example, in a herd of cows none of the animals is a sheep, therefore the herd itself is not sheep. In the same way, in the collection of the body and mind, neither the body nor the mind is the I, therefore the collection itself is not the I.

4 If the I is not the body, not the mind, and not the collection of the body and mind, the only possibility that remains is that it is something separate from the body and mind. If this is the case, we must be able to apprehend the I without either the body or the mind appearing, but if we imagine that our body and our mind were completely to disappear there would be nothing remaining that could be called the I. Therefore it follows that the I is not separate from the body and mind.

We should imagine that our body gradually dissolves into thin air, and then our mind dissolves, our thoughts scatter with the wind, our feelings, wishes, and awareness melt into nothingness. Is there anything left that is the I? There is nothing. Clearly the I is not something separate from the body and mind.

We have now examined all four possibilities and have failed to find the I. Since we have already decided that there is no fifth possibility, we must conclude that the truly existent, or inherently existent, I that normally appears so vividly does not exist at all. Where there previously appeared an inherently existent I, there now appears an absence of that I. This absence of an inherently existent I is emptiness, ultimate truth.

We contemplate in this way until there appears to our mind a generic image of the absence of an inherently existent I. This image is our object of placement meditation. We try to become completely familiar with it by concentrating on it single-pointedly for as long as possible.

Because we have grasped at an inherently existent I since beginningless time, and have cherished it more dearly than anything else, the experience of failing to find the I in meditation can be quite shocking at first. Some people develop fear, thinking that they have become completely non-existent. Others feel great joy, as if the source of all their problems is vanishing. Both reactions are good signs and indicate correct meditation. After a while these initial reactions will subside and our mind will settle into a more balanced state. Then we shall be able to meditate on emptiness in a calm, controlled manner.

We should allow our mind to become absorbed in space-like emptiness for as long as possible. It is important to remember that our object is emptiness, the absence of an inherently existent I, not mere nothingness. Occasionally we should check our meditation with alertness. If our mind has wandered to another object, or if we have lost the meaning of emptiness and are focusing on mere nothingness, we should return to the contemplations to bring emptiness clearly to mind once again.

We may wonder: 'If there is no truly existent I, then who is meditating? Who will get up from meditation, speak to others, and reply when my name is called?' Though there is nothing within the body and mind, or separate from the body and mind, that is the I, this does not mean that the I does not exist at all. Although the I does not exist in any of the four ways mentioned above, it does exist conventionally. The I is merely a designation imputed by conceptual mind upon the collection of the body and mind. So long as we are satisfied with the mere designation 'I', there is no problem. We can think 'I exist', 'I am going to town', and so on. The problem arises only when we look for an I other than the mere conceptual imputation, 'I'. The self-grasping mind grasps at an I that ultimately exists, independent of conceptual imputation, as if there were a 'real' I existing behind the label. If such an I existed we would be able to find it, but we have seen that the I cannot be found upon investigation. The conclusion of our search was a definite non-finding of the I. This unfindability of the I is the emptiness of the I, the ultimate nature of the I. The I that exists as mere imputation is the conventional nature of the I.

When we first realize emptiness we do so conceptually, by means of a generic image. By continuing to meditate on emptiness over and over again, the generic image gradually becomes more and more transparent until it disappears entirely and we see emptiness directly. This direct realization of emptiness will be our first completely non-mistaken awareness, or 'undefiled' mind. Until we realize emptiness directly all our minds are mistaken awarenesses because, due to the imprints of self-grasping or true-grasping ignorance, their objects appear as inherently existent.

Most people veer towards the extreme of existence, thinking that if something exists it must exist inherently, thus exaggerating the way in which things exist without being satisfied with them as mere name. Others may veer towards the extreme of non-existence, thinking that if phenomena do not exist inherently they do not exist at all, thus exaggerating their lack of inherent existence. We need to realize that although phenomena lack any trace of existence

Khädrub Tendzin Tsöndru

from their own side, they do exist conventionally as mere appearances to a valid mind.

The conceptual minds grasping at the I and other phenomena as being truly existent are wrong awarenesses and should therefore be abandoned, but I am not saying that all conceptual thoughts are wrong awarenesses and should therefore be abandoned. There are many correct conceptual minds that are useful in our day-to-day lives, such as the conceptual mind remembering what we did yesterday or the conceptual mind understanding how to make a cup of tea. There are also many conceptual minds that need to be cultivated on the spiritual path. For example, conventional bodhichitta in the mental continuum of a Bodhisattva is a conceptual mind because it apprehends its object, great enlightenment, by means of a generic image. Moreover, before we can realize emptiness directly with a nonconceptual mind, we need to realize it by means of an inferential cognizer, which is a conceptual mind. Through contemplating the reasons that refute inherent existence there appears to our mind a generic image of the absence, or emptiness, of inherent existence. This is the only way that emptiness of inherent existence can initially appear to our mind. We then meditate on this image with stronger and stronger concentration until finally we perceive emptiness directly.

There are some people who say that the way to meditate on emptiness is simply to empty our mind of all conceptual thoughts, arguing that just as white clouds obscure the sun as much as black clouds, so positive conceptual thoughts obscure our mind as much as negative conceptual thoughts.

This view is completely mistaken, for if we make no effort to gain a conceptual understanding of emptiness but try instead to suppress all conceptual thoughts, actual emptiness will never appear to our mind. We may achieve a vivid experience of a space-like vacuity, but this is just the absence of conceptual thought – it is not emptiness, the true nature of phenomena. Meditation on this vacuity may temporarily calm our mind, but it will never destroy our delusions nor liberate us from samsara.

If all the necessary atmospheric causes and conditions come together, clouds will appear. If these are absent, clouds cannot form. The clouds are completely dependent upon causes and conditions for their development; without these they have no power to develop. The same is true for mountains, planets, bodies, minds and all other produced phenomena. Because they depend upon factors outside themselves for their existence, they are empty of inherent, or independent, existence and are mere imputations of the mind.

Contemplating the teachings on karma can help us to understand this. Where do all our good and bad experiences come from? According to Buddhism they are the result of the positive and negative karma we created in the past. As a result of positive karma, attractive and agreeable people appear in our life, pleasant material conditions arise, and we live in a beautiful environment; but as a result of negative karma unpleasant people and things appear. This world is the effect of the collective karma created by the beings who inhabit it. Because karma originates in the mind – specifically in our mental intentions – we can see that all worlds arise from the mind. This is similar to the way in which appearances arise in a dream. Everything we perceive when we are dreaming is the result of the ripening of karmic potentials in our mind and has no existence outside of our mind. When our mind is calm and pure, positive karmic imprints ripen and pleasant dream appearances arise; but when our mind is agitated and impure, negative karmic imprints ripen and unpleasant, nightmarish appearances arise. In a similar way, all the appearances of our waking world are simply the ripening of positive, negative or neutral karmic imprints in our mind.

Once we understand how things arise from their inner and outer causes and conditions and have no independent existence, then just seeing or thinking about the production of phenomena will remind us of their emptiness. Instead of reinforcing our sense of the solidity and objectivity of things, we shall begin to see things as manifestations of their emptiness, with no more concrete existence than a rainbow arising out of an empty sky.

Just as the production of things depends upon causes and conditions, so too does the disintegration of things. Therefore neither production nor disintegration can be truly existent. For example, if our new car was destroyed we would feel unhappy because we grasp at both the car and the disintegration of the car as truly existent; but if we understood that our car is merely an appearance to our mind, like a car in a dream, its destruction would not disturb us. This is true for all objects of our attachment; if we realize that both objects and their cessations lack true

existence there is no basis for becoming upset if we are separated from them.

All functioning things – our environments, enjoyments,
body, mind and self – change from moment to moment.
They are impermanent in the sense that they do not last for
a second moment. The book you are reading in this moment
is not the same book that you were reading a moment ago,
and it could only come into existence because the book of a
moment ago ceased to exist. When we understand subtle
impermanence – that our body, mind, self and so forth do
not abide for a second moment – it is not difficult to understand that they are empty of inherent existence.

Even though we may agree that impermanent phenomena are empty of inherent existence, we might think that
because permanent phenomena are unchanging and do not
arise from causes and conditions they must exist inherently.
However, even permanent phenomena such as emptiness
and unproduced space – the mere absence of physical
obstruction – are dependent-related phenomena because
they depend upon their parts, their bases and the minds
that impute them; and therefore they are not inherently
existent. Although emptiness is ultimate reality, it is not
independent or inherently existent for it too depends upon
its parts, its bases and the minds that impute it. Just as a
gold coin does not exist separately from its gold, so the
emptiness of our body does not exist separately from our
body, because it is simply our body's lack of inherent
existence.

Whenever we go anywhere we develop the thought 'I am
going', and grasp at an inherently existent act of going. In a

similar way, when someone comes to visit us we think 'They are coming', and we grasp at an inherently existent act of coming. Both these conceptions are self-grasping and wrong awarenesses. When someone goes away we feel that a truly existent person has truly left, and when they come back we feel that a truly existent person has truly returned. However, the coming and going of people is like the appearance and disappearance of a rainbow in the sky. When the causes and conditions for a rainbow to appear are assembled a rainbow appears, and when the causes and conditions for the continued appearance of the rainbow disperse the rainbow disappears; but the rainbow does not come from anywhere nor does it go anywhere.

When we observe one object, such as our I, we strongly feel that it is a single, indivisible entity, and that its singularity is inherently existent. In reality, however, our I has many parts, such as the parts that look, listen, walk and think, or the parts that are, for example, a teacher, a mother, a daughter and a wife. Our I is imputed onto the collection of all these parts. As with each individual phenomenon it is a singularity, but its singularity is merely imputed, like an army that is merely imputed onto a collection of soldiers or a forest that is imputed onto a collection of trees.

When we see more than one object we regard the multiplicity of these objects to be inherently existent. However, just as singularity is merely imputed, likewise plurality is just an imputation by mind and does not exist from the side of the object. For example, instead of looking at a collection of soldiers or trees from the point of view of the individual soldiers or trees, we could look at them as an army or a forest, that is, as a singular collection or whole, in which case we would be looking at a singularity rather than a plurality.

In summary, singularity does not exist from its own side because it is just imputed upon a plurality – its parts. In the same way plurality does not exist from its own side because it is just imputed upon a singularity – the collection of its parts. Therefore singularity and plurality are mere imputations by conceptual mind and they lack true existence. If we realize this clearly, there is no basis for developing attachment and anger towards objects, either singular or plural. We tend to project the faults or qualities of the few onto the many, and then develop hatred or attachment on the basis of, for example, race, religion or country. Contemplating the emptiness of singularity and plurality can be helpful in reducing such hatred and attachment.

Although production, disintegration and so forth do exist, they do not exist inherently or truly, and the conceptual minds that grasp them as truly existent are instances of self-grasping ignorance. These conceptions grasp at the eight extremes: truly existent production, truly existent disintegration, truly existent impermanence, truly existent permanence, truly existent going, truly existent coming, truly existent singularity and truly existent plurality. Although these extremes do not exist, due to our ignorance we are always grasping them. The conceptions of these extremes lie at the root of all delusions, and because delusions give rise to contaminated actions that keep us trapped in samsara, these conceptions are the root of samsara.

The subject of the eight extremes is profound and requires detailed explanation and lengthy study. Buddha explains them in detail in the *Perfection of Wisdom Sutras*; and in *Fundamental Wisdom*, a commentary to the *Perfection of Wisdom Sutras*, Nagarjuna also uses many profound and powerful reasons to prove that the eight extremes do not exist by showing how all phenomena are empty of inherent existence. Through analyzing conventional truths he establishes their ultimate nature, and shows why it is necessary to understand both the conventional and ultimate natures of an object in order to understand that object fully.

CONVENTIONAL AND ULTIMATE TRUTHS

Whatever exists is either a conventional truth or an ultimate truth, and, since ultimate truth refers just to emptiness, everything except emptiness is a conventional truth. The things that we see directly, such as houses, cars and tables, are all conventional truths.

All conventional truths are false objects because the way they appear and the way they exist do not correspond. If someone appears to be friendly and kind but his real intention is to gain our confidence in order to rob us, we would say that he is false or deceptive because there is a discrepancy between the way he appears and his real nature. Similarly, objects such as forms and sounds are false or deceptive because they appear to exist inherently but in reality are completely devoid of inherent existence. Because the way they appear does not coincide with the way they

Dorjechang Phabongkha Trinlay Gyatso

exist, conventional truths are known as 'deceptive phenomena'. A cup, for instance, appears to exist independently of its parts, its causes, and the mind that apprehends it, but in reality it totally depends upon these things. Because the way the cup appears to our mind and the way it exists do not correspond, the cup is a false object.

Although conventional truths are false objects nevertheless they actually exist because a mind directly perceiving a conventional truth is a valid mind, a completely reliable mind. For instance, an eye consciousness directly perceiving a cup on the table is a valid mind because it will not deceive us – if we reach out to pick up the cup we shall find it where our eye consciousness sees it. In this respect an eye consciousness perceiving a cup on the table is different from an eye consciousness mistaking a cup reflected in a mirror for a real cup, or an eye consciousness seeing a mirage as water. Even though a cup is a false object, for practical purposes the eye consciousness that directly perceives it is a valid, reliable mind. However, although it is a valid mind it is nevertheless mistaken insofar as the cup appears to that mind to be truly existent. It is valid and non-deceptive with respect to the conventional characteristics of the cup – its position, size, colour and so forth – but mistaken with respect to its ultimate nature.

To summarize, conventional objects are false because, although they appear to exist from their own side, in reality they are mere appearances to mind, like things seen in a dream. Within the context of a dream, however, dream objects have a relative validity, and this distinguishes them from things that do not exist at all. Suppose in a dream we steal a diamond and someone then asks us whether it was we who stole it. Even though the dream is merely a creation of our mind, if we answer 'yes' we are telling the truth whereas if we answer 'no' we are telling a lie. In the same way, even though in reality the whole universe is just an appearance to mind, within the context of the experience of ordinary beings we can distinguish between relative truths and relative falsities.

Conventional truths can be divided into gross conventional truths and subtle conventional truths. We can understand how all phenomena have these two levels of conventional truth by considering the example of a car. The car itself, the car depending on its causes, and the car depending on its parts are all gross conventional truths of the car. They are called 'gross' because they are relatively easy to understand. The car depending on its basis of imputation is quite subtle and is not easy to understand, but it is still a gross conventional truth. The basis of imputation of the car is the parts of the car. To apprehend car, the parts of the car must appear to our mind; without the parts appearing there is no way to develop the thought 'car'. For this reason the parts are the basis of imputation of the car. We say 'I see a car', but strictly speaking all we ever see is parts of the car. However, when we develop the thought 'car' by seeing its parts, we see the car. There is no car other than its parts, there is no body other than its parts, and so on. The car existing merely as an imputation by thought is the subtle conventional truth of the car. We have understood this when we realize that the car is nothing more than a mere imputation by a valid mind. We cannot understand subtle conventional truths unless we have understood emptiness. When we thoroughly realize subtle conventional truth we have realized both conventional truth and ultimate truth.

Strictly speaking, truth, ultimate truth and emptiness are synonymous because conventional truths are not real truths but false objects. They are true only for the minds of those who have not realized emptiness. Only emptiness is true because only emptiness exists in the way that it appears. When the mind of any sentient being directly perceives conventional truths, such as forms, they appear to exist from their own side. When the mind of a Superior being directly perceives emptiness, however, nothing appears other than emptiness; this mind is totally mixed with the mere absence of true existence. The way in which emptiness appears to the mind of a non-conceptual direct perceiver corresponds exactly to the way in which emptiness exists.

It should be noted that although emptiness is ultimate truth it is not inherently existent. Emptiness is not a separate reality existing behind conventional appearances, but the real nature of those appearances. We cannot talk about emptiness in isolation, for emptiness is always the mere lack of inherent existence *of* something. For example, the emptiness of our body is the lack of inherent existence of our body, and without our body as its basis this emptiness cannot exist. Because emptiness necessarily depends upon a basis, it lacks inherent existence.

In *Guide to the Bodhisattva's Way of Life* Shantideva defines ultimate truth as a phenomenon that is true for the uncontaminated mind of a Superior being. An uncontaminated mind is a mind that realizes emptiness directly. This mind is the only unmistaken awareness and is possessed exclusively by Superior beings. Because uncontaminated minds are completely unmistaken, anything directly perceived by them to be true is necessarily an ultimate truth. In contrast, anything that is directly perceived to be true by the mind of an ordinary being is necessarily not an ultimate truth, because all minds of ordinary beings are mistaken, and mistaken minds can never directly perceive the truth.

Due to the imprints of conceptual thoughts that grasp at the eight extremes, everything that appears to the minds of ordinary beings appears to be inherently existent. Only the wisdom of meditative equipoise that directly realizes emptiness is undefiled by the imprints, or stains, of these conceptual thoughts. This is the only wisdom that has no mistaken appearance.

When a Superior Bodhisattva meditates on emptiness his or her mind mixes with emptiness completely, with no appearance of inherent existence. He develops a completely pure, uncontaminated wisdom that is ultimate bodhichitta. When he arises from meditative equipoise, however, due to the imprints of true-grasping conventional phenomena again appear to his mind as inherently existent, and his uncontaminated wisdom temporarily becomes non-manifest. Only a Buddha can manifest uncontaminated wisdom at the same time as directly perceiving conventional truths. An uncommon quality of a Buddha is that a single moment of a Buddha's mind realizes both conventional truth and ultimate truth directly and simultaneously. There are many levels of ultimate bodhichitta. For instance, the ultimate bodhichitta attained through Tantric practice is more profound than that developed through Sutra practice alone, and the supreme ultimate bodhichitta is that of a Buddha.

If through valid reasoning we realize the emptiness of the first extreme, the extreme of production, we shall easily be able to realize the emptiness of the remaining seven extremes. Once we have realized the emptiness of the eight extremes we have realized the emptiness of all phenomena. Having gained this realization, we continue to contemplate and meditate on the emptiness of produced phenomena and so forth, and as our meditations deepen we shall feel all phenomena dissolving into emptiness. We shall then be able to maintain a single-pointed concentration on the emptiness of all phenomena.

To meditate on the emptiness of produced phenomena we can think:

There is an I or self that is reborn again and again within samsara. This I is a produced phenomenon because its existence depends upon causes and conditions, such as its previous continuum and our karma, and therefore it lacks true existence. If we search for our I within our body and mind, or separate from our body and mind, we cannot find it; and instead of a truly existent I appearing to our mind a space-like emptiness appears.

We feel that our mind enters into this space-like emptiness and remains there single-pointedly. In this way we try to maintain continuously the appearance of the emptiness of inherent existence of the I. What appears to our mind is just a space-like emptiness, but we understand this emptiness to

161

be the non-existence of the truly existent I. We need to maintain both the appearance of emptiness and the special understanding of the meaning of this emptiness. This meditation is called 'space-like meditative equipoise on emptiness'.

Just as eagles soar through the vast expanse of the sky without meeting any obstructions, needing only minimal effort to maintain their flight, so advanced meditators concentrating on emptiness can meditate on emptiness for a long time with little effort. Their minds soar through space-like emptiness, undistracted by any other phenomenon. When we meditate on emptiness we should try to emulate these meditators. Once we have found our object of meditation, the mere absence of the inherently existent I, we should refrain from further analysis and simply rest our mind in the experience of this emptiness. From time to time we should check to make sure that we have lost neither the clear appearance of emptiness nor the recognition of its meaning, but we should not check too forcefully as this will disturb our concentration. Our meditation should not be like the flight of a small bird, which never stops flapping its wings and is always changing direction, but like the flight of an eagle, which soars gently with only occasional adjustments to its wings. Through meditating in this way we shall feel our mind dissolving into and becoming one with emptiness.

If we are successful in doing this, then during our meditation we are free from manifest self-grasping. If on the other hand we spend all our time checking and analyzing, never allowing our mind to relax into the space of emptiness, we shall never gain this experience and our meditation will not serve to reduce our self-grasping.

In general we need to improve our understanding of emptiness through extensive study, approaching it from many angles and using many different lines of reasoning. It is also important to become thoroughly familiar with one complete meditation on emptiness through continuous contemplation, understanding exactly how to use the reasoning to lead to an experience of emptiness. We can then concentrate on emptiness single-pointedly and try to mix our mind with it, like water mixing with water.

THE UNION OF THE TWO TRUTHS

The union of the two truths means that conventional truths, such as our body, and ultimate truths, such as the emptiness of our body, are the same nature. The main purpose of understanding and meditating on this union is to prevent dualistic appearances – appearances of inherent existence to the mind that is meditating on emptiness – and thereby enable our mind to dissolve into emptiness. Once we can do this our meditation on emptiness will be very powerful in eliminating our delusions. If we correctly identify and negate the inherently existent body, and meditate on the mere absence of such a body with strong concentration, we shall feel our normal body dissolving into emptiness. We shall understand that the real nature of our body is emptiness and that our body is merely a manifestation of emptiness.

Emptiness is like the sky and our body is like the blue of the sky. Just as the blue is a manifestation of the sky itself and cannot be separated from it, so our blue-like body is simply a manifestation of the sky of its emptiness and cannot be separated from it. If we realize this, when we focus on the emptiness of our body we feel that our body itself dissolves into its ultimate nature. In this way we can easily overcome the conventional appearance of the body in our meditations, and our mind naturally mixes with emptiness.

In the *Heart Sutra* Bodhisattva Avalokiteshvara says 'Form is not other than emptiness'. This means that conventional phenomena, such as our body, do not exist separately from their emptiness. When we meditate on the emptiness of our body with this understanding, we know that the emptiness appearing to our mind is the very nature of our body, and that apart from this emptiness there is no body. Meditating in this way will greatly weaken our self-grasping mind. If we really believed that our body and its emptiness were the same nature, our self-grasping would definitely become weaker.

Although we can divide emptinesses from the point of view of their bases, and speak of the emptiness of the body, the emptiness of the I and so forth, in truth all emptinesses are the same nature. If we look at ten bottles we can distinguish ten different spaces inside the bottles, but in reality these spaces are the same nature; and if we break the bottles the spaces become indistinguishable. In the same way, although we can speak of the emptiness of the body, the mind, the I and so forth, in reality they are the same nature and indistinguishable. The only way in which they can be distinguished is by their conventional bases.

There are two principal benefits of understanding that all emptinesses are the same nature: in the meditation session our mind will mix with emptiness more easily, and in the meditation break we shall be able to see all appearances as equal manifestations of their emptiness.

For as long as we feel that there is a gap between our mind and emptiness – that our mind is 'here' and emptiness is 'there' – our mind will not mix with emptiness. Knowing that all emptinesses are the same nature helps to close this gap. In ordinary life we experience many different objects – good, bad, attractive, unattractive – and our feelings towards them differ. Because we feel that the differences exist from the side of the objects, our mind is unbalanced and we develop attachment to attractive objects, aversion to unattractive objects, and indifference to neutral objects. It is very difficult to mix such an uneven mind with emptiness. To mix our mind with emptiness we need to know that although phenomena appear in many different aspects, in essence they are all empty. The differences we see are just appearances to mistaken minds; from the point of view of ultimate truth all phenomena are equal in emptiness. For a qualified meditator single-pointedly absorbed in emptiness, there is no difference between production and disintegration, impermanence and permanence, going and coming, singularity and plurality – everything is equal in emptiness and all problems of attachment, anger and self-grasping ignorance are solved. In this experience everything becomes very peaceful and comfortable, balanced and

Yongdzin Dorjechang Losang Yeshe

harmonious, joyful and wonderful. There is no heat, no cold, no lower, no higher, no here, no there, no self, no other, no samsara – everything is equal in the peace of emptiness. This realization is called the 'yoga of equalizing samsara and nirvana', and is explained in detail in both the Sutras and Tantras.

Since all emptinesses are the same nature, the ultimate nature of a mind that is meditating on emptiness is the same nature as the ultimate nature of its object. When we first meditate on emptiness our mind and emptiness appear to be two separate phenomena, but when we understand that all emptinesses are the same nature we shall know that this feeling of separation is simply the experience of a mistaken mind. In reality our mind and emptiness are ultimately of one taste. If we apply this knowledge in our meditations it will help to prevent the appearance of the conventional nature of our mind and allow our mind to dissolve into emptiness.

Having mixed our mind with emptiness, when we arise from meditation we shall experience all phenomena equally as manifestations of their emptiness. Instead of feeling that the attractive, unattractive and neutral objects we see are inherently different, we shall know that in essence they are the same nature. Just as both the gentlest and most violent waves in an ocean are equally water, likewise both attractive forms and repulsive forms are equally manifestations of emptiness. Realizing this, our mind will become balanced and peaceful. We shall recognize all conventional appearances as the magical play of the mind, and we shall not grasp strongly at their apparent differences.

When Milarepa once taught emptiness to a woman he compared emptiness to the sky and conventional truths to clouds and told her to meditate on the sky. She followed his instructions with great success, but she had one problem – when she meditated on the sky of emptiness, everything disappeared and she could not understand how phenomena could exist conventionally. She said to Milarepa: 'I find it easy to meditate on the sky but difficult to establish the clouds. Please teach me how to meditate on the clouds.' Milarepa replied: 'If your meditation on the sky is going well, the clouds will not be a problem. Clouds simply appear in the sky – they arise from the sky and dissolve back into the sky. As your experience of the sky improves, you will naturally come to understand the clouds.'

In Tibetan the word for both sky and space is 'namkha', although space is different from sky. There are two types of space, produced space and unproduced space. Produced space is the visible space we can see inside a room or in the sky. This space may become dark at night and light during the day, and as it undergoes change in this way it is an impermanent phenomenon. The characteristic property of produced space is that it does not obstruct objects – if there is space in a room we can place objects there without obstruction. Similarly birds are able to fly through the space of the sky because it lacks obstruction, whereas they cannot fly through a mountain! Therefore it is clear that produced space lacks, or is empty of, obstructive contact. This mere lack, or emptiness, of obstructive contact is unproduced space.

Because unproduced space is the mere absence of obstructive contact it does not undergo momentary change and is therefore a permanent phenomenon. Whereas produced space is visible and quite easy to understand, unproduced space is a mere absence of obstructive contact and is rather more subtle. However, once we understand unproduced space we shall find it easier to understand emptiness.

The only difference between emptiness and unproduced space is their object of negation. The object of negation of unproduced space is obstructive contact whereas the object of negation of emptiness is inherent existence. Because unproduced space is the best analogy for understanding emptiness, it is used in the Sutras and in many scriptures. Unproduced space is a non-affirming negative phenomenon – a phenomenon that is realized by a mind that merely eliminates its negated object without realizing another positive phenomenon. Produced space is an affirmative, or positive, phenomenon – a phenomenon that is realized without the mind explicitly eliminating a negated object. More details on these two types of phenomenon can be found in *Ocean of Nectar*.

THE PRACTICE OF EMPTINESS IN OUR DAILY ACTIVITIES

In our daily activities we should regard all appearances as illusory. Although things appear to us as inherently existent we should remember that these appearances are deceptive and that in reality things lack true existence. When a magician creates an illusory tiger, a tiger appears very clearly to his mind but he knows that it is just an illusion. Indeed, the very appearance of the tiger reminds him that there is no tiger. In the same way, when we are very familiar with emptiness the very fact that things appear to be truly existent will remind us that they are not truly existent. We should therefore recognize that whatever appears to us in our daily life is like an illusion and lacks true existence. In this way our wisdom will increase day by day, and our self-grasping ignorance and other delusions will naturally diminish.

Between meditation sessions we should be like an actor. When an actor plays the part of a king he dresses, speaks and acts like a king, but he knows all the time that he is not a real king. In the same way we should live and function in the conventional world yet always remember that we ourself, our environment, and the people around us are not the truly existent entities they seem to be. They are merely projections of our mind, and their real nature is just emptiness.

If we think like this we shall be able to live in the conventional world without grasping at it. We shall treat it lightly, and have the flexibility of mind to respond to every situation in a constructive way. Knowing that whatever appears to our mind is mere appearance, when attractive objects appear we shall not grasp at them and develop attachment, and when unattractive objects appear we shall not grasp at them and develop aversion or anger.

In *Training the Mind in Seven Points* Geshe Chekhawa says: 'Think that all phenomena are like dreams.' Some of the things we see in our dreams are beautiful and some are ugly, but they are all mere appearances to our dreaming mind. They do not exist from their own side, and are empty of inherent existence. It is the same with the objects we perceive when we are awake – they too are mere appearances to mind and lack inherent existence.

All phenomena lack inherent existence. When we look at a rainbow it appears to occupy a particular location in space, and it seems that if we searched we would be able to find where the rainbow touches the ground. However, we know that no matter how hard we search we shall never be able to find the end of the rainbow, for as soon as we arrive at the place where we saw the rainbow touch the ground, the rainbow will have disappeared. If we do not search for it the rainbow appears clearly, but when we look for it it is not there. All phenomena are like this. If we do not analyze them they appear clearly, but when we search for them analytically, trying to isolate them from everything else, they are not there.

If something did exist inherently, and we investigated it by separating it from all other phenomena, we would be able to find it. However, all phenomena are like rainbows – if we search for them we shall never find them. At first we might find this idea very uncomfortable and difficult to accept, but this is quite natural. With greater familiarity we shall find this reasoning more acceptable, and eventually we shall realize that it is true.

It is important to understand that emptiness does not mean nothingness. Although things do not exist from their own side, independent of the mind, they do exist in the

Dorjechang Kelsang Gyatso Rinpoche

sense that they are understood by a valid mind. The world we experience when we are awake is similar to the world we experience when we are dreaming. We cannot say that dream things do not exist, but if we believe that they exist as more than mere appearances to the mind, existing 'out there', then we are mistaken, as we shall discover when we wake up.

There is no greater method for experiencing peace of mind and happiness than to understand and meditate on emptiness. Since it is our self-grasping that keeps us bound to the prison of samsara and is the source of all our suffering, meditation on emptiness is the universal solution to all our problems. It is the medicine that cures all mental and physical diseases and the nectar that bestows the everlasting happiness of nirvana and enlightenment.

As explained earlier, Mahamudra Tantra is a single mind that has two parts: (1) experiencing great bliss, and (2) realizing emptiness directly. We can accomplish the first part through Buddha's Tantric teachings – presented in the first two parts of this book – and we can accomplish the second part through Buddha's Sutra teachings – presented in this Part Three. Through this we shall attain the realization of Mahamudra Tantra, which gives inconceivable meaning to our life.

Dedication

Through the power of the virtues accumulated by writing this book, may all sufferings quickly cease, may all happiness and joy be fulfilled, and may holy Dharma flourish for evermore.

Appendix I

The Root Tantra of
Heruka and Vajrayogini

Introduction

The *Heruka Root Tantras* belong to the Highest Yoga Tantra of Vajrayana Buddhism. Buddha taught the extensive, middling and condensed *Heruka Root Tantras*. The *Condensed Heruka Root Tantra*, which has fifty-one chapters, was translated from Sanskrit into Tibetan.

Commentaries to the *Condensed Heruka Root Tantra* given by Buddha Shakyamuni, and many other commentaries written by Indian Buddhist Masters such as Mahasiddhas Naropa and Lawapa, were also translated. Later commentaries were written by Tibetan Tantric scholars based on Je Tsongkhapa's commentary to the *Condensed Heruka Root Tantra* entitled *Clear Illumination of All Hidden Meanings*.

I have translated the first and last chapters of the *Condensed Heruka Root Tantra* from Tibetan into English. As Je Tsongkhapa said, each word of the root Tantra has many different meanings; I have translated the hidden meaning, not the words. My purpose in doing this is to benefit the people of this modern world.

Geshe Kelsang Gyatso, 2003.

The Root Tantra of
Heruka and Vajrayogini

Spoken by the Blessed One, Buddha Shakyamuni, at the request of Vajrapani.

Thus I shall explain the great secret –
The instructions on the stages of Heruka's path –
The unsurpassed of all the unsurpassed
That fulfils the wish for all attainments.

Generate the Pure Land of Heruka with the celestial
    mansion,
And yourself as glorious Buddha Heruka embracing
    Vajravarahi
With a retinue of thirty-six Dakinis and twenty-four Heroes;
In the supreme secret of great bliss
Always gather the nature of all.
Thus Heruka, who is imputed upon this great bliss,
Which is inseparable from the emptiness of all,
Is the Blessed One, definitive Heruka,
The synthesis of all Dakas and Dakinis.

And Heruka who appears with a blue-coloured body
With four faces and twelve arms,
Is the interpretative Heruka taught for commitment.
The supreme secret of great bliss
Arises through melting the drops inside the central
    channel;
Thus it is hard to find in the world
A person who experiences such bliss.
When examined there is no body;
You should know all things in the same way.
The commitments, meditations, recitations,
And other rituals will be explained.

Practitioners should always make offerings,
Either extensively or briefly,
To the assembly of Deities of Heruka's mandala,
Especially on the tenth and twenty-fifth days of each month.
With the motivation of the compassionate mind of
    bodhichitta
And the wisdom realizing the emptiness of all phenomena,
A practitioner can rely upon the three messengers –
An emanation, one who possesses realizations, or
One who is keeping the commitments purely.
The bliss arising through melting your own drops
Should be offered to Heruka who abides at your heart.
Because Heruka is always at the practitioner's heart,
Inseparable from him or her,
Anyone who sees, hears, touches or remembers such a
    practitioner
Will definitely receive Heruka's blessings.

Practitioners have the great power to heal themselves
And to accumulate merit and wisdom;
They can quickly accomplish attainments
Through meditation and recitation of the mantras.
As a basic practice you should always keep the
    commitments;
Breaking these would destroy the blessings
That you received when granted the empowerment,
And thus you would not accomplish any attainments.
Bliss through melting the drops inside the central channel,
Mixed completely with the emptiness of all,
Is the supreme secret of great bliss
That gives rise to all five attainments –
Pacifying, increasing and controlling attainments,
Attainments through wrathful actions,
And the attainment of supreme enlightenment.

By penetrating the point of the lower tip of your central
    channel,
When joined with the lower tip of the central channel of
    the mudra,
Wisdom wind will enter your central channel;
Through gaining deep experience with this meditation
You will attain the supreme secret of great bliss.
You can also rely on and practise the four mudras –
Commitment, action, phenomenon and great;
The four different ways of embracing should be known.
The bliss experienced by such a pure practitioner
Is unequalled by any bliss experienced by gods or
    humans.

The place where you meditate on the great secret
Can be a mountain, forest, cemetery, town or city.
Having found a suitable place with no obstacles
You should continually strive to accomplish
The supporting and supported mandala of Heruka.

This concludes Chapter One: *The Condensation of the Heruka Root Tantra.*

The other instructions, which are hard to find,
That are hidden in the scriptures –
The way to accomplish the mandalas of Heruka –
Will also be briefly explained.

To begin, you should meditate on the meaning of Shri
   Heruka,
The union of great bliss and emptiness.
Then, meditate on the correct imaginations that believe:
The place is the actual Pure Land of Heruka
Appearing in the aspect of the supporting mandala,
The protection circle and celestial mansion;
Your body is the supreme secret of great bliss
Appearing in the form of Heruka's blue-coloured body,
Adorned with the five ornaments
And embracing the wisdom consort Vajravarahi;
Your speech is the nature of the mantra of AHLIKALI,
The source of all the mantras;
You are receiving the blessings and empowerment;
Your body is adorned with the inner protection,
The protection circle of the armour mantras;
The Deities of the five wheels appear in the celestial
   mansion;
The migrators of the six realms are purified
By emanating rays of wisdom light;
Outer, inner and eight-line mantra offerings are made;
Training in clear appearance and divine pride
Beyond ordinary appearance and conceptions –
Thus I have explained the fourteen essential points.

Those who sincerely engage in this practice
Will quickly purify all negativities,
Always take higher rebirth with good fortune,
And attain the state of the Conqueror Buddha.

Just as fire quickly destroys objects,
The recitations and meditations of Heruka and
    Vajrayogini
Quickly destroy suffering.
When such practitioners experience death,
Various emanations will appear to them
With offerings such as flowers and beautiful music,
And lead them to the Pure Land of Keajra.
For such practitioners, death is just mere name –
They are simply moved from the prison of samsara
To the Pure Land of Buddha Heruka.
The good fortune of Heruka Tantra practice
Will be extremely hard to find in the future –
Thus you should not waste the opportunity you have
    now.
The twelve arms of Heruka indicate that the practitioner
    will be freed
From the twelve dependent-related links of samsara;
Treading on Bhairawa and Kalarati shows victory over
    the maras –
Thus you should strive to practise these instructions.
Generate yourself as the principal of the mandala,
Surrounded by the Heroes and Yoginis of the five wheels
Who are all delighted with the supreme secret of great
    bliss.

At the end of the session, the supporting and supported
All dissolve into great bliss and emptiness –
Meditate on this union of bliss and emptiness.
From this, arise as the action Deity Heruka
Who engages in subsequent practices.

The Blessed One appears in many different aspects
To benefit all living beings who have different wishes.
Among the various methods that the Blessed One has
    shown
To fulfil the various wishes of living beings,
Supreme are the instructions of Sutra and the four classes
    of Tantra –
Action, Performance, Yoga and Highest Yoga Tantra.
You should never abandon Highest Yoga Tantra,
But realize that it has inconceivable meaning
And is the very essence of Buddhadharma.
It is hard to understand the profound meaning of Highest
    Yoga Tantra
For those who do not understand the real nature of
    things, emptiness.
However, the emanations of Buddha Vajradhara pervade
    everywhere
And the Buddha lineage of all beings is always with
    them;
Thus finally all living beings without exception
Will attain the supreme state of enlightenment,
    Buddhahood.

This concludes Chapter Fifty-One: *The Conclusion of the
Heruka Root Tantra.*

The condensed mantra of Heruka, Vajrayogini, the thirty-six Dakinis and the twenty-four Heroes

OM HUM BAM RIM RIM LIM LIM, KAM KHAM GAM GHAM
NGAM, TSAM TSHAM DZAM DZHAM NYAM, TrAM THrAM
DrAM DHrAM NAM, TAM THAM DAM DHAM NAM, PAM
PHAM BAM BHAM, YAM RAM LAM WAM, SHAM KAM SAM
HAM HUM HUM PHAT

For the sake of all living beings,
May I become Heruka;
And then lead every living being
To Heruka's supreme state.

Colophon: This text was translated by
Venerable Geshe Kelsang Gyatso.

Appendix II

An Explanation of Channels

An Explanation of Channels

There are three main channels: the central channel, the right channel and the left channel. The central channel is like the pole of an umbrella, running through the centre of each of the channel wheels, and the other two run either side of it. The central channel is pale blue and has four attributes: (1) it is very straight, like the trunk of a plantain tree, (2) inside it has an oily red colour, like pure blood, (3) it is very clear and transparent, like a candle flame, and (4) it is very soft and flexible, like a lotus petal.

The central channel is located exactly midway between the left and right halves of the body, but is closer to the back than the front. Immediately in front of the spine, there is the life channel, which is quite thick; and in front of this is the central channel. As mentioned before, it begins at the point between the eyebrows, from where it ascends in an arch to the crown of the head and then descends in a straight line to the tip of the sex organ. Although its most common name is the central channel, it is also known as the 'two abandonments' because gathering the winds into this channel causes the negative activity associated with the winds of the right and left channels to be abandoned. It is also known as the 'mind channel' and as 'Rahu'.

Either side of the central channel, with no intervening space, are the right and left channels. The right channel is red in colour and the left is white. The right channel begins at the tip of the right nostril and the left channel at the tip of the left nostril. From there they both ascend in an arch to the crown of the head, either side of the central channel. From the crown of the head down to the navel, these three major channels are straight and adjacent to one another. As the left channel continues down below the level of the navel, it curves a little to the right, separating slightly from the central channel and rejoining it at the tip of the sex organ. There it functions to hold and release sperm, blood, and urine. As the right channel continues down below the level of the navel, it curves a little to the left and terminates at the tip of the anus, where it functions to hold and release faeces and so forth.

Other names for the right channel are the 'sun channel', the 'speech channel' and the 'channel of the subjective holder'. This last title indicates that the winds flowing through this channel cause the generation of conceptions developed in terms of the subjective mind. Other names for the left channel are the 'moon channel', the 'body channel' and the 'channel of the held object', with the last title indicating that the winds flowing through this channel cause the generation of conceptions developed in terms of the object.

The right and left channels coil around the central channel at various places, thereby forming the so-called 'channel knots'. The four places at which these knots occur are, in ascending order, the navel channel wheel, the heart channel wheel, the throat channel wheel and the crown channel wheel. At each of these places, except at the heart level, there is one twofold knot formed by a single coil of the right channel and a single coil of the left. As the right and left channels ascend to these places, they coil around the central channel by crossing in front and then looping around it. They then continue upward to the level of the next knot. At the heart level, the same thing happens, except that here there is a six-fold knot formed by three overlapping loops of each of the flanking channels.

The four places where these knots occur are four of the six major channel wheels. At each of the six major channel wheels, a different number of spokes, or petals, branch off from the central channel in the same way that the ribs of an umbrella appear to branch off from the central pole. Thus, at the crown channel wheel (known as the 'great bliss wheel') there are thirty-two such petals or channel spokes, all of them white in colour. The centre is triangular with the apex facing forwards. (This refers to the shape of the coiled knot through which the spokes emanate, as seen from the top.) These thirty-two spokes arch downwards, like the ribs of an upright umbrella. A description of this and the three other major channel wheels where knots occur is given in Chart 1.

Chart 1 The Four Major Channel Wheels

location	name	shape of centre	number of spokes	colour	direction of arching
crown	great bliss wheel	triangular	thirty-two	white	downwards
throat	enjoyment wheel	circular	sixteen	red	upwards
heart	Dharma wheel	circular	eight	white	downwards
navel	emanation wheel	triangular	sixty-four	red	upwards

These four channel wheels contain a total of one hundred and twenty spokes. As for the remaining two major channel wheels, the channel wheel at the secret place has thirty-two red-coloured spokes arching downwards and the jewel channel wheel has eight white spokes arching upwards. It should also be noted that according to some texts the spokes at the crown, navel and secret place can be visualized as having various colours.

Since the heart channel wheel is of particular importance, it will now be described in more detail. Its eight spokes, or petals, are arranged in the cardinal and intermediate directions with the front being the east. In each spoke, there flows mainly the supporting wind of a particular element as indicated in Chart 2.

Chart 2 The Spokes of the Heart Channel Wheel

direction	supporting wind
east	of the earth element
north	of the wind element
west	of the fire element
south	of the water element
south-east	of the element of form
south-west	of the element of smell
north-west	of the element of taste
north-east	of the element of touch

From each of these eight petals or channel spokes of the heart, three channels split off, making twenty-four channels in all. These are the channels of the twenty-four places. They are all included in three groups of eight: the channels of the mind wheel, which are blue and contain mainly winds; the channels of the speech wheel, which are red and contain mostly red drops; and the channels of the body wheel, which are white and contain mostly white drops. Each channel goes to a different place in the body. These places are the twenty-four inner places. When we practise the extensive Heruka sadhana, we visualize the Deities of the body mandala at these places.

The outer tips of the eight channels of the mind wheel terminate at: (1) the hairline, (2) the crown, (3) the right ear,

(4) the back of the neck, (5) the left ear, (6) the brow (the place between the eyebrows), (7) the two eyes, and (8) the two shoulders. Those of the speech wheel terminate at: (9) the two armpits, (10) the two breasts, (11) the navel, (12) the tip of the nose, (13) the mouth, (14) the throat, (15) the heart (the area midway between the two breasts), and (16) the two testicles or the two sides of the vagina. Finally, those of the body wheel terminate at: (17) the tip of the sex organ, (18) the anus, (19) the two thighs, (20) the two calves, (21) the eight fingers and eight lesser toes, (22) the tops of the feet, (23) the two thumbs and the two big toes, and (24) the two knees.

Each of these twenty-four channels splits into three branches, which are distinguished by the principal elements – winds, red drops and white drops – that flow through them. Each of these seventy-two channels then splits into a thousand, making seventy-two thousand channels in all. It is important for a Highest Yoga Tantric practitioner to be familiar with the arrangement of the channels since it is through gaining control over the winds and drops flowing through these channels that the union of spontaneous great bliss and emptiness is accomplished.

The winds in the body of an ordinary person flow through most of these channels except the central channel. Because these winds are impure, the various minds that they support are also impure, and so for as long as these winds continue to flow through the peripheral channels they will continue to support the various negative conceptions that keep us trapped in samsara. Through the force of meditation, however, these winds can be brought into the central channel, where they are no longer able to support the development of gross conceptions of dualistic appearance. With a mind free from dualistic appearances, we shall be able to gain a direct realization of ultimate truth, emptiness.

Corresponding to the twenty-four inner places of the Heruka body mandala are the 'twenty-four outer places', which are located at various points throughout this world. Practitioners with pure karma can see these outer places of Heruka as Pure Lands, but people with impure karma see them only as ordinary places.

Appendix III

An Explanation of Inner Winds

An Explanation of Inner Winds

The definition of wind is any of the four elements that is light in weight and moving. Winds can be divided into external and internal winds, and into gross and subtle winds. Gross external wind is the wind we experience on a windy day. Subtle external wind is much more difficult to detect. It is the energy that makes plants grow and exists even inside rocks and mountains. It is with the help of subtle winds that plants draw up water, grow new leaves, and so forth. Such winds are the life-force of plants. Indeed, in some Tantric texts wind is called 'life' or 'life-force'. Thus, although it is incorrect to say that plants are alive in the sense of being conjoined with consciousness, we can say that they are alive in this sense.

Internal winds are the winds in the continuum of a person that flow through the channels of the body. The main function of internal winds is to move the mind to its object. The function of the mind is to apprehend objects, but without a wind to act as its mount it cannot move towards, or

Chart 3 The Root Winds

	life-supporting	downward-voiding	upward-moving	equally-abiding	pervading
colour	white	yellow	red	green/yellow	pale blue
Buddha family	Akshobya	Ratnasambhava	Amitabha	Amoghasiddhi	Vairochana
element	water	earth	fire	wind	space
seat	heart	the two lower doors: the anus and the sex organ	throat	navel	both the upper and lower parts of the body, mainly the 360 joints
function	to support and maintain life	to retain and release urine, faeces, semen, blood, etc.	to speak, swallow, etc.	to cause the inner fire to blaze, to digest food and drink, etc.	to enable the body to come and go; to allow movement, lifting, and placing
direction	from both nostrils, gently downwards	from both nostrils, horizontally heavily forwards	from the right nostril, violently upwards	from the left nostril, moving to the left and the right from the edge of this nostril	this wind does not flow through the channels except at the moment of death

establish a connection with, its object. Mind is sometimes likened to a lame person who can see, and wind to a blind person with legs. It is only by operating together with internal winds that minds can function.

There are many different winds flowing through the channels of the body, but all are included within the five root winds and the five branch winds. The five root winds are:

1 The life-supporting wind
2 The downward-voiding wind
3 The upward-moving wind
4 The equally-abiding wind
5 The pervading wind

Each of the five root winds has six characteristics by which it can be recognized: (1) its colour, (2) its associated Buddha family, (3) an element for which it serves as the support, (4) its principal seat or fundamental location, (5) its function, and (6) its direction (how it leaves the nostrils upon exhalation). These are summarized in Chart 3.

The life-supporting wind is called the 'Akshobya wind' because, when it is completely purified, it transforms into the nature of Akshobya. At the moment, our life-supporting wind is like the seed of Akshobya's Form Body, but not Akshobya himself. The main function of the life-supporting wind is to support life by maintaining the connection between body and mind. The stronger the life-supporting wind, the longer we shall live. Another function of this wind is to support the water element of our body and to cause it to increase. The life-supporting wind is white in colour and its principal location is at the heart. When we exhale, it leaves from both nostrils, flowing gently downwards.

The downward-voiding wind is the seed of Ratna-sambhava's Form Body and is associated with the earth element. It is yellow in colour and it functions to release urine, faeces, sperm, and menstrual blood. Its principal locations are at the anus and the sex organ, and when we exhale, it leaves horizontally from both nostrils, flowing heavily forwards.

The upward-moving wind is the seed of Amitabha's Form Body and is associated with the fire element. It is red in colour and it functions to enable us to swallow food and drink, to speak, to cough and so forth. Its principal location is at the throat, and when we exhale it leaves from the right nostril, flowing violently upwards.

The equally-abiding wind is the seed of Amoghasiddhi's Form Body and is associated with the wind element. It is greenish-yellow in colour and it functions to cause the inner fire to blaze, and to digest food and drink by separating the nutrients from waste matter. Its principal location is at the navel, and when we exhale it leaves from the left nostril, moving to the left and the right from the edge of the nostril.

The pervading wind is the seed of Vairochana's Form Body and is associated with the space element. It is pale blue in colour and, as its name suggests, it pervades the entire body, particularly the three hundred and sixty joints. It functions to enable the body to move. Without this wind we would be completely immobile, like a stone. This wind does not flow through the nostrils except at the moment of death.

Generally speaking, at any one time, one of the winds is flowing more strongly through the nostrils than the other winds. If, for example, the life-supporting wind is flowing strongly, the other winds (except the pervading wind) are flowing gently. Unless we observe our breath very carefully, it is difficult to notice the different movements of the four winds, but they definitely flow through our nostrils whenever we breath.

The five branch winds are:

1 The moving wind
2 The intensely-moving wind
3 The perfectly-moving wind
4 The strongly-moving wind
5 The definitely-moving wind

The five branch winds are so called because they branch off from the life-supporting wind, which resides in the heart centre. The main location of these winds is in the four channel spokes of the heart channel wheel, from where they flow through our channels to the five doors of the sense powers. Because they function to enable sense awarenesses to develop, the five branch winds are also called the 'five winds of the sense powers'. The colour and function of each branch wind are summarized in Chart 4.

Chart 4 The Branch Winds

name	colour	function
the moving wind	red	to enable the eye awareness to move to visual forms
the intensely-moving wind	blue	to enable the ear awareness to move to sounds
the perfectly-moving wind	yellow	to enable the nose awareness to move to smells
the strongly-moving wind	white	to enable the tongue awareness to move to tastes
the definitely-moving wind	green	to enable the body awareness to move to tactile objects

The first wind, the moving wind, flows from the heart through the door of the eyes to enable the eye awareness to move to its object, visual forms. Without the moving wind, eye awareness would be powerless to contact visual forms. The reason we cannot see when we are asleep is that the moving wind has withdrawn from the door of the eye sense power back to its seat at the heart.

The intensely-moving wind flows from the heart to the ears, enabling the ear awareness to move to sounds; the perfectly-moving wind flows from the heart to the nostrils, enabling the nose awareness to move to smells; the strongly-moving wind flows from the heart to the tongue, enabling the tongue awareness to move to tastes; and the definitely-moving wind flows from the heart all over the body, enabling the body awareness to move to tactile objects.

The downward-voiding wind, the upward-moving wind, the equally-abiding wind, the pervading wind, and the five branch winds are all gross internal winds. The life-supporting wind has three levels: gross, subtle and very subtle. Most mounted winds of conceptual thoughts are gross life-supporting winds; the mounted winds of the minds of white appearance, red increase and black near-attainment are subtle life-supporting winds; and the mounted wind of the mind of clear light is a very subtle life-supporting wind.

The life-supporting wind is very extensive. If a defiled life-supporting wind manifests, negative conceptual thoughts will develop, but if the life-supporting wind is purified, negative conceptual thoughts will be pacified. All meditations use the mental awareness, and the mounted wind of mental awareness is necessarily a life-supporting wind.

Each of the five winds of the sense powers and the gross life-supporting wind has two parts: a wind that develops the specific type of awareness, and a wind that moves the awareness towards its object. These twelve winds normally flow through the right and left channels, and are the principal objects to be purified by means of vajra recitation, as explained in *Tantric Grounds and Paths* and *Essence of Vajrayana*. If we want to overcome distractions, it is very important to cause these twelve winds to enter, abide and dissolve within the central channel.

Appendix IV

Vajra Hero Yoga

A BRIEF ESSENTIAL PRACTICE OF
HERUKA BODY MANDALA SELF-GENERATION

&

CONDENSED SIX-SESSION YOGA

Introduction

Those who are unable to recite the extensive sadhana, *Essence of Vajrayana*, can begin with this brief essential yoga of Heruka body mandala self-generation. The detailed meaning of this practice should be understood from the extensive sadhana and its commentary, *Essence of Vajrayana*.

It is most important to improve our faith and conviction in this practice through careful reading of its commentary. With a clear understanding and strong faith we can enjoy this very essential practice of Highest Yoga Tantra and attain the ultimate goal of human life.

Vajra Hero Yoga

THE PRELIMINARY PRACTICES

Visualizing the objects of refuge and the Field of Merit

In the space before me appear Guru Heruka Father and Mother, surrounded by the assembly of direct and lineage Gurus, Yidams, Buddhas, Bodhisattvas, Heroes, Dakinis, and Dharma Protectors.

Going for refuge and generating aspiring bodhichitta

Eternally I shall go for refuge
To Buddha, Dharma, and Sangha.
For the sake of all living beings
I shall become Heruka.   (3x)

Generating engaging bodhichitta

To lead all mother living beings to the state of ultimate
  happiness,
I shall attain as quickly as possible, in this very life,
The state of the Union of Buddha Heruka.
For this purpose I shall practise the stages of Heruka's
  path.   (3x)

Guru yoga

Prayer of seven limbs

With my body, speech, and mind, humbly I prostrate,
And make outer, inner, and secret offerings.
I confess my wrong deeds from all time,
And rejoice in the virtues of all.
Please stay until samsara ceases,
And turn the Wheel of Dharma for us.
I dedicate all virtues to the great enlightenment of
  Heruka.

Offering the mandala

The ground sprinkled with perfume and spread with
  flowers,
The Great Mountain, four lands, sun and moon,
Seen as a Buddha Land and offered thus,
May all beings enjoy such Pure Lands.

I offer without any sense of loss
The objects that give rise to my attachment, hatred, and
    confusion,
My friends, enemies, and strangers, our bodies and
    enjoyments;
Please accept these and bless me to be released directly
    from the three poisons.

IDAM GURU RATNA MANDALAKAM NIRYATAYAMI

Requesting our root Guru

As times become ever more impure
Your power and blessings ever increase,
And you care for us quickly, as swift as thought;
O my root Guru Heruka Father and Mother, please
    bestow your blessings.   (3x)

**Accomplishing spontaneous great bliss by dissolving
    the Guru into oneself**

The Field of Merit gathers gradually from the edges and
dissolves into my root Guru Heruka. Out of delight he
comes to my crown, descends through my central
channel, and becomes of one taste with my mind at my
heart. I experience spontaneous great bliss.

THE ACTUAL PRACTICE OF GENERATION STAGE

Bringing death into the path of the Truth Body

Light rays from the HUM at my heart melt all worlds and beings into light. This dissolves into me, and I in turn gradually melt into light from below and above and dissolve into the HUM at my heart. The letter HUM dissolves in stages from the bottom up into the nada. The nada becomes smaller and smaller and dissolves into clear light emptiness. I am Truth Body Heruka.

Bringing the intermediate state into the path of the Enjoyment Body

From the state of emptiness my mind appears in the form of a nada. I am Enjoyment Body Heruka.

Bringing rebirth into the path of the Emanation Body

From YAM, RAM, BAM, LAM, SUM, PAM arise the four elements, Mount Meru, and the lotus. In the centre of the lotus, from the vowels and consonants, arises a reddish-white moon, the nature of the red and white bodhichittas of Guru Heruka Father and Mother. I, the nada, enter the centre of the moon and gradually transform into the aspect of a HUM.

Five-coloured lights radiate from the HUM and lead all living beings to the state of Chakrasambara. At the same time all the Heroes and Heroines are invited from the Buddha Lands of the ten directions. They all melt into light and dissolve into the HUM, which becomes the nature of spontaneous joy. The moon, vowels, consonants, and HUM completely transform, and the Deities of the body mandala together with the mandala arise fully and all at once. I am Emanation Body Heruka.

Thus I am Heruka with a blue-coloured body, four faces, and twelve arms, the nature of my white indestructible drop. I am embracing Vajravarahi, the nature of my red indestructible drop. I am surrounded by the Heroes and Heroines of the five wheels, who are the nature of my purified channels and drops. I reside in the mandala, the celestial mansion, which is the nature of my purified gross body.

Inviting the wisdom beings, dissolving them into the commitment beings, and receiving the empowerment

PHAIM

My three places are marked by the three letters. Light rays radiate from the letter HUM and invite all the Buddhas of the ten directions in the same aspect as those visualized, together with the empowering Deities. All the wisdom beings gather into one complete supporting and supported mandala.

DZA HUM BAM HO

The wisdom beings become inseparable from the commitment beings.

The empowering Deities grant the empowerment, my body is filled with nectar, and I experience bliss. The excess nectar on the crowns completely transforms, and the Principal is adorned by Vajrasattva, Vajravarahi by Akshobya, the four Mothers by Ratnasambhava, the Deities of the heart wheel by Akshobya, the Deities of the speech wheel by Amitabha, the Deities of the body wheel by Vairochana, and the Deities of the commitment wheel by Amoghasiddhi.

Making offerings and praise to the self-generated Deities of the body mandala

Countless breathtakingly beautiful offering and praising goddesses emanate from my heart and make offerings and praise to me as Heruka Father and Mother.

Outer offerings

OM AHRGHAM PARTITZA SÖHA
OM PADÄM PARTITZA SÖHA
OM ÄNTZAMANAM PARTITZA SÖHA
OM VAJRA PUPE AH HUM SÖHA
OM VAJRA DHUPE AH HUM SÖHA
OM VAJRA DIWE AH HUM SÖHA
OM VAJRA GÄNDHE AH HUM SÖHA
OM VAJRA NEWIDE AH HUM SÖHA
OM VAJRA SHAPTA AH HUM SÖHA

OM AH VAJRA ADARSHE HUM
OM AH VAJRA WINI HUM

OM AH VAJRA GÄNDHE HUM
OM AH VAJRA RASE HUM
OM AH VAJRA PARSHE HUM
OM AH VAJRA DHARME HUM

Inner offering

OM HUM BAM RIM RIM LIM LIM, KAM KHAM GAM GHAM
NGAM, TSAM TSHAM DZAM DZHAM NYAM, TRAM THRAM
DRAM DHRAM NAM, TAM THAM DAM DHAM NAM, PAM
PHAM BAM BHAM, YAM RAM LAM WAM, SHAM KAM SAM
HAM HUM HUM PHAT OM AH HUM

Secret and thatness offerings

I, the Principal Father and Mother, enter into the union of
embrace. The bodhichitta melts, and as it descends from
my crown to my throat I experience joy, as it descends
from my throat to my heart I experience supreme joy, as
it descends from my heart to my navel I experience
extraordinary joy, and as it descends from my navel to
the tip of my jewel I generate spontaneous great bliss
inseparable from emptiness. The Principal and all the
retinue experience a special, exalted wisdom of bliss and
emptiness.

Praise

To Glorious Heruka Father and Mother,
The nature of all the Buddhas' compassion,
And to all the Heroes and Heroines of the five wheels,
Respectfully I prostrate.

*At this point, (1) while experiencing great bliss and empti-
ness, (2) we meditate on the clear appearance of the mandala
and Deities, and (3) we meditate on divine pride, while (4)
recognizing that the Deities are the nature of our purified
channels and drops, and that the mandala is the nature of
our purified gross body.*

*In this way we train sincerely in one single concentration
on gross or subtle generation stage possessing these four
characteristics. Holding the fourth characteristic – recognizing the Deities as the nature of our purified channels and
drops, and the mandala as the nature of our purified gross
body – makes this concentration an actual body mandala
meditation.*

*Then, when we need to rest from meditation, we can prac-
tise mantra recitation.*

Blessing the mala

The mala becomes emptiness. From the state of emptiness
each bead appears in its own aspect, the nature of
Pämanarteshvara, the vajra speech of all Buddhas.

Mantra recitation

Visualization

The mantra to be recited descends from the letter HUM at
my heart, leaves through the tip of my vajra, enters the
consort's bhaga, ascends, leaves through her mouth,
enters my mouth, descends, and dissolves back into
the HUM. Then again it circles as before, leaving and

re-entering my central channel. My four mouths, and all
the Deities of the retinue, recite the mantras.

Recite the following mantras as many times as you can:

The essence mantra of the Father

OM SHRI VAJRA HE HE RU RU KAM HUM HUM PHAT DAKINI
   DZALA SHAMBARAM SÖHA

The close essence mantra of the Father

OM HRIH HA HA HUM HUM PHAT

The essence mantra of the Mother

OM VAJRA BEROTZANIYE HUM HUM PHAT SÖHA

The close essence mantra of the Mother

OM SARWA BUDDHA DAKINIYE VAJRA WARNANIYE HUM
   HUM PHAT SÖHA

The condensed essence mantra of the sixty retinue
   Deities

OM RIM RIM LIM LIM, KAM KHAM GAM GHAM NGAM, TSAM
TSHAM DZAM DZHAM NYAM, TrAM THrAM DrAM DHrAM
NAM, TAM THAM DAM DHAM NAM, PAM PHAM BAM BHAM,
YAM RAM LAM WAM, SHAM KAM SAM HAM HUM HUM PHAT

*At this point you can, if you wish, make torma offerings and
tsog offerings. These can be found in the extensive sadhana,*
Essence of Vajrayana.

Dedication

Thus, through my virtues from correctly performing the
   offerings, praises, recitations, and meditations
Of the generation stage of Glorious Heruka,
May I complete all the stages
Of the common and uncommon paths.

For the sake of all living beings
May I become Heruka;
And then lead every living being
To Heruka's supreme state.

And if I do not attain this supreme state in this life,
At my deathtime may I be met by the venerable Father
   and Mother and their retinue,
With clouds of breathtaking offerings, heavenly music,
And many excellent, auspicious signs.

Then, at the end of the clear light of death,
May I be led to Pure Dakini Land,
The abode of the Knowledge Holders who practise the
   supreme path;
And there may I swiftly complete this profound path.

May the most profound practice and instruction of Heruka,
Practised by millions of powerful Yogis greatly increase;
And may it remain for a very long time without degenerating,
As the main gateway for those seeking liberation.

May the Heroes, Dakinis, and their retinues
Abiding in the twenty-four supreme places of this world,
Who possess unobstructed power for accomplishing this
    method,
Never waver from always assisting practitioners.

Auspicious prayers

May there be the auspiciousness of a great treasury of
    blessings
Arising from the excellent deeds of all the root and
    lineage Gurus,
Who have accomplished the supreme attainment of
    Buddha Heruka
By relying upon the excellent, secret path of the King of
    Tantras.

May there be the auspiciousness of the great excellent
    deeds of the Three Jewels –
The holy Buddha Jewel, the pervading nature Heruka;
The ultimate, great, secret Dharma Jewel, the scriptures
    and realizations of Heruka Tantra;
And the supreme Sangha Jewel, the assemblies of
    Heruka's retinue Deities.

Through all the great good fortune there is
In the precious, celestial mansions as extensive as the
    three thousand worlds,
Adorned with ornaments like the rays of the sun and the
    moon,
May all worlds and their beings have happiness,
    goodness, glory, and prosperity.

Prayers for the Virtuous Tradition

So that the tradition of Je Tsongkhapa,
The King of the Dharma, may flourish,
May all obstacles be pacified
And may all favourable conditions abound.

Through the two collections of myself and others
Gathered throughout the three times,
May the doctrine of Conqueror Losang Dragpa
Flourish for evermore.

The nine-line *Migtsema* prayer

Tsongkhapa, crown ornament of the scholars of the Land
of the Snows,
You are Buddha Shakyamuni and Vajradhara, the source
of all attainments,
Avalokiteshvara, the treasury of unobservable
compassion,
Manjushri, the supreme stainless wisdom,
And Vajrapani, the destroyer of the hosts of maras.
O Venerable Guru-Buddha, synthesis of all Three Jewels,
With my body, speech, and mind, respectfully I make
requests:
Please grant your blessings to ripen and liberate myself
and others,
And bestow the common and supreme attainments.

(3x)

Condensed Six-session Yoga

*Everyone who has received a Highest Yoga Tantra empower-
ment has a commitment to practise six-session Guru yoga. If
we are very busy we can fulfil our six-session commitment
by doing the following practice six times each day. First we
recall the nineteen commitments of the five Buddha families
that are listed below, and then, with a strong determination
to keep these commitments purely, we recite the* Condensed
Six-session Yoga *that follows.*

THE NINETEEN COMMITMENTS OF
THE FIVE BUDDHA FAMILIES

The six commitments of the family of Buddha Vairochana

1 To go for refuge to Buddha
2 To go for refuge to Dharma
3 To go for refuge to Sangha
4 To refrain from non-virtue
5 To practise virtue
6 To benefit others

The four commitments of the family of Buddha Akshobya

1 To keep a vajra to remind us of great bliss
2 To keep a bell to remind us of emptiness
3 To generate ourself as the Deity
4 To rely sincerely upon our Spiritual Guide

The four commitments of the family of Buddha Ratnasambhava

1 To give material help
2 To give Dharma
3 To give fearlessness
4 To give love

The three commitments of the family of Buddha Amitabha

1 To rely upon the teachings of Sutra
2 To rely upon the teachings of the two lower classes of Tantra
3 To rely upon the teachings of the two higher classes of Tantra

The two commitments of the family of Buddha Amoghasiddhi

1 To make offerings to our Spiritual Guide
2 To strive to maintain purely all the vows we have taken

CONDENSED SIX-SESSION YOGA

I go for refuge to the Guru and Three Jewels.
Holding vajra and bell I generate as the Deity and make offerings.
I rely upon the Dharmas of Sutra and Tantra and refrain from all non-virtuous actions.
Gathering all virtuous Dharmas, I help all living beings through the practice of the four givings.

All nineteen commitments are referred to in this verse. The words, 'I go for refuge to the ... Three Jewels', refer to the first three commitments of the family of Buddha Vairochana – to go for refuge to Buddha, to go for refuge to Dharma, and to go for refuge to Sangha. The word, 'Guru', *refers to the fourth commitment of the family of Buddha Akshobya – to rely sincerely upon our Spiritual Guide.*

The words, 'Holding vajra and bell I generate as the Deity', *refer to the first three commitments of the family of Buddha Akshobya – to keep a vajra to remind us of great bliss, to keep a bell to remind us of emptiness, and to generate ourself as the Deity. The words,* 'and make offerings', *refer to the first commitment of the family of Buddha Amoghasiddhi – to make offerings to our Spiritual Guide.*

The words, 'I rely upon the Dharmas of Sutra and Tantra', *refer to the three commitments of the family of Buddha Amitabha – to rely upon the teachings of Sutra, to rely upon the teachings of the two lower classes of Tantra, and to rely upon the teachings of the two higher classes of Tantra. The words,* 'and refrain from all non-virtuous actions', *refer to the fourth commitment of the family of Buddha Vairochana – to refrain from non-virtue.*

The words, 'Gathering all virtuous Dharmas', *refer to the fifth commitment of the family of Buddha Vairochana – to practise virtue. The words,* 'I help all living beings', *refer to the sixth commitment of the family of Buddha Vairochana – to benefit others. The words,* 'through the practice of the four givings', *refer to the four commitments of the family of Buddha Ratnasambhava – to give material help, to give Dharma, to give fearlessness, and to give love.*

Finally, the entire verse refers to the second commitment of the family of Buddha Amoghasiddhi – to strive to maintain purely all the vows we have taken.

More details on the vows and commitments of Secret Mantra can be found in the book Tantric Grounds and Paths.

Colophon: This sadhana was compiled from traditional sources by Venerable Geshe Kelsang Gyatso.

Appendix V

Heart Jewel

THE GURU YOGA OF JE TSONGKHAPA
COMBINED WITH THE CONDENSED
SADHANA OF HIS DHARMA PROTECTOR

Liberating Prayer

PRAISE TO BUDDHA SHAKYAMUNI

O Blessed One, Shakyamuni Buddha,
Precious treasury of compassion,
Bestower of supreme inner peace,

You, who love all beings without exception,
Are the source of happiness and goodness;
And you guide us to the liberating path.

Your body is a wishfulfilling jewel,
Your speech is supreme, purifying nectar,
And your mind is refuge for all living beings.

With folded hands I turn to you,
Supreme unchanging friend,
I request from the depths of my heart:

Please give me the light of your wisdom
To dispel the darkness of my mind
And to heal my mental continuum.

Please nourish me with your goodness,
That I in turn may nourish all beings
With an unceasing banquet of delight.

Through your compassionate intention,
Your blessings and virtuous deeds,
And my strong wish to rely upon you,

May all suffering quickly cease
And all happiness and joy be fulfilled;
And may holy Dharma flourish for evermore.

This prayer was composed by Venerable Geshe Kelsang Gyatso.
It is recited regularly at the beginning of sadhanas in
Kadampa Buddhist Centres throughout the world.

Introduction

This sadhana includes two practices revealed by the Wisdom Buddha Manjushri. The first is a special Guru yoga in which we visualize our Spiritual Guide as Je Tsongkhapa, who himself is a manifestation of Manjushri. By relying upon this practice, we can purify negativity, accumulate merit, and receive blessings. In this way, we will naturally accomplish all the realizations of the stages of the path of Sutra and Tantra, and in particular we will attain a very special Dharma wisdom.

The second practice is a method for relying upon the Dharma Protector Dorje Shugdän. Through this, we can overcome obstacles to our practice and create favourable conditions so that we can nurture and increase our Dharma realizations. If we rely upon the Dharma Protector Dorje Shugdän sincerely, our faith in Je Tsongkhapa will naturally increase and we will easily gain experience of the pure Buddhadharma transmitted directly to Je Tsongkhapa by the Wisdom Buddha Manjushri.

These two practices are the very essence of the New Kadampa Tradition of Mahayana Buddhism. If we practise them regularly and sincerely, we will reap a rich harvest of pure Dharma realizations, and eventually come to experience the supreme joy of full enlightenment.

An extensive explanation of this sadhana can be found in the book entitled *Heart Jewel*.

Heart Jewel

Going for refuge

I and all sentient beings, until we achieve enlightenment,
Go for refuge to Buddha, Dharma, and Sangha.   (3x)

Generating bodhichitta

Through the virtues I collect by giving and other
    perfections,
May I become a Buddha for the benefit of all.   (3x)

Inviting Je Tsongkhapa

From the heart of the Protector of the hundreds of Deities
    of the Joyful Land,
To the peak of a cloud which is like a cluster of fresh,
    white curd,
All-knowing Losang Dragpa, King of the Dharma,
Please come to this place together with your Sons.

Prayer of seven limbs

In the space before me on a lion throne, lotus, and moon,
The venerable Gurus smile with delight.
O Supreme Field of Merit for my mind of faith,
Please remain for a hundred aeons to spread the doctrine.

Your mind of wisdom realizes the full extent of objects of
    knowledge,
Your eloquent speech is the ear-ornament of the fortunate,
Your beautiful body is ablaze with the glory of renown,
I prostrate to you, whom to see, to hear, and to remember
    is so meaningful.

Pleasing water offerings, various flowers,
Sweet-smelling incense, lights, scented water, and so
    forth,
A vast cloud of offerings both set out and imagined,
I offer to you, O Supreme Field of Merit.

Whatever non-virtues of body, speech, and mind
I have accumulated since time without beginning,
Especially transgressions of my three vows,
With great remorse I confess each one from the depths of
    my heart.

In this degenerate age you strove for much learning and
    accomplishment.
Abandoning the eight worldly concerns, you made your
    freedom and endowment meaningful.
O Protector, from the very depths of my heart,
I rejoice in the great wave of your deeds.

From the billowing clouds of wisdom and compassion
In the space of your Truth Body, O Venerable and holy
    Gurus,
Please send down a rain of vast and profound Dharma
Appropriate to the disciples of this world.

Through the virtues I have accumulated here,
May the doctrine and all living beings receive every
    benefit.
Especially may the essence of the doctrine
Of Venerable Losang Dragpa shine forever.

Offering the mandala

The ground sprinkled with perfume and spread with
    flowers,
The Great Mountain, four lands, sun and moon,
Seen as a Buddha Land and offered thus,
May all beings enjoy such Pure Lands.

IDAM GURU RATNA MANDALAKAM NIRYATAYAMI

Migtsema prayer

Tsongkhapa, crown ornament of the scholars of the Land
    of the Snows,
You are Avalokiteshvara, the treasury of unobservable
    compassion,
Manjushri, the supreme stainless wisdom,
And Vajrapani, the destroyer of the hosts of maras;
O Losang Dragpa I request you, please grant your
    blessings.   (7x, 21x, 100x, etc.)

Prayer of the Stages of the Path

The path begins with strong reliance
On my kind Teacher, source of all good;
O Bless me with this understanding
To follow him with great devotion.

This human life with all its freedoms,
Extremely rare, with so much meaning;
O Bless me with this understanding
All day and night to seize its essence.

My body, like a water bubble,
Decays and dies so very quickly;
After death come results of karma,
Just like the shadow of a body.

With this firm knowledge and remembrance
Bless me to be extremely cautious,
Always avoiding harmful actions
And gathering abundant virtue.

Samsara's pleasures are deceptive,
Give no contentment, only torment;
So please bless me to strive sincerely
To gain the bliss of perfect freedom.

O Bless me so that from this pure thought
Come mindfulness and greatest caution,
To keep as my essential practice
The doctrine's root, the Pratimoksha.

Just like myself all my kind mothers
Are drowning in samsara's ocean;
O So that I may soon release them,
Bless me to train in bodhichitta.

But I cannot become a Buddha
By this alone without three ethics;
So bless me with the strength to practise
The Bodhisattva's ordination.

By pacifying my distractions
And analyzing perfect meanings,
Bless me to quickly gain the union
Of special insight and quiescence.

When I become a pure container
Through common paths, bless me to enter
The essence practice of good fortune,
The supreme vehicle, Vajrayana.

The two attainments both depend on
My sacred vows and my commitments;
Bless me to understand this clearly
And keep them at the cost of my life.

By constant practice in four sessions,
The way explained by holy Teachers,
O Bless me to gain both the stages,
Which are the essence of the Tantras.

May those who guide me on the good path,
And my companions all have long lives;
Bless me to pacify completely
All obstacles, outer and inner.

May I always find perfect Teachers,
And take delight in holy Dharma,
Accomplish all grounds and paths swiftly,
And gain the state of Vajradhara.

Receiving blessings and purifying

From the hearts of all the holy beings, streams of light and nectar flow down, granting blessings and purifying.

Requests to receive the Guru's blessings

O Glorious and precious root Guru,
Please sit on the lotus and moon seat at my heart.
Please care for me with your great kindness,
And grant me the blessings of your body, speech, and
    mind.

O Glorious and precious root Guru,
Please sit on the lotus and moon seat at my heart.
Please care for me with your great kindness,
And bestow the common and supreme attainments.

O Glorious and precious root Guru,
Please sit on the lotus and moon seat at my heart.
Please care for me with your great kindness,
And remain firm until I attain the essence of
    enlightenment.

Dedication

Through being cared for throughout all my lives
By Conqueror Tsongkhapa as my Mahayana Guru,
May I never turn away, even for an instant,
From this excellent path praised by the Conquerors.

Inviting Dorje Shugdän and his retinue

HUM
I have the clarity of the Yidam.
Before me in the centre of red and black fire and wind,
On a lotus and sun, trampling demons and obstructors,
Is a terrifying lion, which is powerful and alert.
Upon this sits the great king Dorje Shugdän,
The supreme Heart Jewel of Dharma Protectors.
His body is clothed in the garments of a monk,
And on his head he wears a round, yellow hat.
His hands hold a sword and a heart of compassion.
To his followers he shows an expression of delight,
But to subdue demons and obstructors he displays a
    wrathful manner.
He is surrounded by a vast, assembled retinue,
Such as his attendant Khache Marpo and so forth.

Light rays from my heart instantly invite the wisdom
beings from the sphere of nature, and from all the
different palaces where they abide. They become
inseparable from the commitment beings.

Making offerings and requests

HUM
Respectfully I prostrate with body, speech, and mind.
I offer a mass of inner and outer offerings, blissful
    tormas,
Alcohol, tea, cakes, milk, and curd,
Both actually set out and mentally imagined, filling the
    whole of space.

Commitment, fulfilling, reliance, and appropriate
    substances,
Outer, inner, secret, attractive, and cleansing offerings,
    filling the whole of space,
I offer these to the entire assembly;
May I fulfil the heart commitment and restore my broken
    commitments.

All my harmful thoughts and actions
That have offended your mind, O Great Protector,
I confess from the depths of my heart.
Please purify them swiftly, and care for me with love, like
    a mother for her child.

I beseech you from the depths of my heart, O Supreme
    Deity,
Please cause the tradition of Je Tsongkhapa to flourish,
Extend the life and activities of the glorious Gurus,
And increase the study and practice of Dharma within
    the Dharma communities.

Please be with me always like the shadow of my body,
And grant me your unwavering care and protection.
Destroy all obstacles and adverse conditions,
Bestow favourable conditions, and fulfil all my wishes.

Now is the time to show clearly your versatile strength
Through your four actions, which are swift, incisive, and
    unobstructed,
To fulfil quickly my special heartfelt desires
In accordance with my wishes;

Now is the time to distinguish the truth and falsity of
    actions and effects;
Now is the time to dispel false accusations against the
    innocent;
Now is the time to protect the pitiful and protectorless;
Now is the time to protect Dharma practitioners as your
    children.

In short, from now until I attain the essence of
    enlightenment,
I shall honour you as the embodiment of my Guru, Deity,
    and Protector.
Therefore please watch over me during the three periods
    of the day and the night
And never waver in your actions as my Protector.

Requesting the fulfilment of wishes

HUM

Whenever your followers with commitments
Request any of the four actions,
Swiftly, incisively, and without delay, you show signs for
all to see;
So please accomplish the actions that I now request of
you.

The stainless sun of Je Tsongkhapa's tradition
Shines throughout the sky of samsara and nirvana,
Eliminating the darkness of inferior and wrong paths;
Please cause its light to spread and bring good fortune to
all living beings.

May the glorious Gurus who uphold this tradition
Have indestructible lives, as stable as the supreme victory
banner;
May they send down a rain of deeds fulfilling the wishes
of disciples,
So that Je Tsongkhapa's doctrine will flourish.

Through increasing the study, practice, pure discipline,
and harmony
Of the communities who uphold the stainless doctrine of
Buddha,
And who keep moral discipline with pure minds,
Please cause the Gedän tradition to increase like a waxing
moon.

Through your actions please fulfil the essential wishes
Of all practitioners who uphold the victory banner
Of practising single-pointedly the stages of the paths of
    Sutra and Tantra,
The essence of all the teachings they have heard.

Beings throughout this great earth are engaged in
    different actions
Of Dharma, non-Dharma, happiness, suffering, cause and
    effect;
Through your skilful deeds of preventing and nurturing,
Please lead all beings into the good path to ultimate
    happiness.

In particular, please destroy the obstacles and
    unfavourable conditions
Of myself and other practitioners.
Increase our lives, our merit, and our resources,
And gather all things animate and inanimate to be freely
    enjoyed.

Please be with me always like the shadow of my body,
And care for me always like a friend,
By accomplishing swiftly whatever I wish for,
And whatever I ask of you.

Please perform immediately, without delaying for a year,
    or even for a month,
Appropriate actions to eliminate all obstacles
Caused by misguided beings with harmful minds who
    try to destroy Je Tsongkhapa's doctrine,
And especially by those who try to harm practitioners.

Please remain in this place always, surrounded by most
    excellent enjoyments.
As my guest, partake continuously of tormas and offerings;
And since you are entrusted with the protection of
    human wealth and enjoyments,
Never waver as my guardian throughout the day and the
    night.

All the attainments I desire
Arise from merely remembering you.
O Wishfulfilling Jewel, Protector of the Dharma,
Please accomplish all my wishes.   (3x)

Dedication

By this virtue may I quickly
Attain the enlightened state of the Guru,
And then lead every living being
Without exception to that ground.

Through my virtues from practising with pure
    motivation,
May all living beings throughout all their lives
Never be parted from peaceful and wrathful Manjushri,
But always come under their care.

Prayers for the Virtuous Tradition

So that the tradition of Je Tsongkhapa,
The King of the Dharma, may flourish,
May all obstacles be pacified
And may all favourable conditions abound.

Through the two collections of myself and others
Gathered throughout the three times,
May the doctrine of Conqueror Losang Dragpa
Flourish for evermore.

The nine-line *Migtsema* prayer

Tsongkhapa, crown ornament of the scholars of the Land
of the Snows,
You are Buddha Shakyamuni and Vajradhara, the source
of all attainments,
Avalokiteshvara, the treasury of unobservable
compassion,
Manjushri, the supreme stainless wisdom,
And Vajrapani, the destroyer of the hosts of maras.
O Venerable Guru-Buddha, synthesis of all Three Jewels,
With my body, speech, and mind, respectfully I make
requests:
Please grant your blessings to ripen and liberate myself
and others,
And bestow the common and supreme attainments.

(3x)

Colophon: This sadhana was compiled from traditional
sources by Venerable Geshe Kelsang Gyatso and
translated under his compassionate guidance.

Glossary

Absorption of cessation An uncontaminated wisdom focused single-pointedly on emptiness in dependence upon the actual absorption of peak of samsara. See *Ocean of Nectar.*

Action mudra A Highest Yoga Tantra consort who assists in developing great bliss. See *Clear Light of Bliss* and *Tantric Grounds and Paths.*

Aggregate In general, all functioning things are aggregates because they are an aggregation of their parts. In particular, a person of the desire realm or form realm has five aggregates: the aggregates of form, feeling, discrimination, compositional factors, and consciousness. A being of the formless realm lacks the aggregate of form but has the other four. A person's form aggregate is his or her body. The remaining four aggregates are aspects of his mind. See also *Contaminated aggregate.* See *Heart of Wisdom.*

Akanishta A Pure Land where Bodhisattvas attain enlightenment. See *Clear Light of Bliss.*

Alertness A mental factor which is a type of wisdom that examines our activity of body, speech, and mind and knows whether or not faults are developing. See *Understanding the Mind.*

Anger A deluded mental factor that observes its contaminated object, exaggerates its bad qualities, considers it to be undesirable, and wishes to harm it. See *Understanding the Mind* and *How to Solve Our Human Problems*.

Atisha (AD 982-1054) A famous Indian Buddhist scholar and meditation master. He was Abbot of the great Buddhist monastery of Vikramashila at a time when Mahayana Buddhism was flourishing in India. He was later invited to Tibet and his arrival there led to the re-establishment of Buddhism in Tibet. He is the author of the first text on the stages of the path, *Lamp for the Path*. His tradition later became known as the 'Kadampa Tradition'. See *Joyful Path of Good Fortune*.

Attachment A deluded mental factor that observes a contaminated object, regards it as a cause of happiness, and wishes for it. See *Understanding the Mind*.

Attainment 'Siddhi' in Sanskrit. These are of two types: common attainments and supreme attainments. Common attainments are of four principal types: pacifying attainments (the ability to purify negativity, overcome obstacles, and cure sickness), increasing attainments (the ability to increase Dharma realizations, merit, lifespan, and wealth), controlling attainments (the ability to control one's own and others' minds and actions), and wrathful attainments (the ability to use wrathful actions where appropriate to benefit others). Supreme attainments are the special realizations of a Buddha. See *Tantric Grounds and Paths*.

Attention A mental factor that functions to focus the mind on a particular attribute of an object. See *Understanding the Mind*.

Avalokiteshvara The embodiment of the compassion of all the Buddhas. Sometimes he appears with one face and four arms, and sometimes with eleven faces and a thousand arms. At the time of Buddha Shakyamuni, he manifested as a Bodhisattva disciple.

Called 'Chenrezig' in Tibetan. See *Living Meaningfully, Dying Joyfully*.

Basis of imputation All phenomena are imputed upon their parts; therefore, any of the individual parts, or the entire collection of the parts, of any phenomenon is its basis of imputation. A phenomenon is imputed by mind in dependence upon its basis of imputation appearing to that mind. See *Heart of Wisdom* and *Ocean of Nectar*.

Beginningless time According to the Buddhist world view, there is no beginning to mind, and so no beginning to time. Therefore, all sentient beings have taken countless previous rebirths.

Bhaga Sanskrit word for the female sex organ.

Blessing 'Jin gyi lab pa' in Tibetan. The transformation of our mind from a negative state to a positive state, from an unhappy state to a happy state, or from a state of weakness to a state of strength, through the inspiration of holy beings such as our Spiritual Guide, Buddhas, and Bodhisattvas.

Bodhichitta Sanskrit term for 'mind of enlightenment'. 'Bodhi' means 'enlightenment', and 'chitta' means 'mind'. There are two types of bodhichitta – conventional bodhichitta and ultimate bodhichitta. Generally speaking, the term 'bodhichitta' refers to conventional bodhichitta, which is a primary mind motivated by great compassion that spontaneously seeks enlightenment to benefit all living beings. There are two types of conventional bodhichitta – aspiring bodhichitta and engaging bodhichitta. Ultimate bodhichitta is a wisdom motivated by conventional bodhichitta that directly realizes emptiness, the ultimate nature of phenomena. See *Joyful Path of Good Fortune* and *Meaningful to Behold*.

Bodhisattva A person who has generated spontaneous bodhichitta but who has not yet become a Buddha. From the moment a practitioner generates a non-artificial, or spontaneous, bodhi-chitta, he or she becomes a Bodhisattva and enters the first Mahayana path, the path of accumulation. An ordinary Bodhisattva is one who has not realized emptiness directly, and a Superior Bodhisattva is one who has attained a direct realization of emptiness. See *Joyful Path of Good Fortune* and *Meaningful to Behold.*

Body mandala The transformation into a Deity of any part of the body of a self-generated or in-front-generated Deity. See *Essence of Vajrayana, Guide to Dakini Land,* and *Great Treasury of Merit.*

Buddha family There are five main Buddha families: the families of Vairochana, Ratnasambhava, Amitabha, Amoghasiddhi, and Akshobya. They are the five purified aggregates – the aggregates of form, feeling, discrimination, compositional factors, and consciousness, respectively; and the five exalted wisdoms – the exalted mirror-like wisdom, the exalted wisdom of equality, the exalted wisdom of individual realization, the exalted wisdom of accomplishing activities, and the exalted wisdom of the Dharmadhatu, respectively. See *Great Treasury of Merit.*

Chandrakirti (circa 7th century AD) A great Indian Buddhist scholar and meditation master who composed, among many other books, the well-known *Guide to the Middle Way,* in which he clearly elucidates the view of the Madhyamika-Prasangika school according to Buddha's teachings given in the *Perfection of Wisdom Sutras.* See *Ocean of Nectar.*

Chekhawa, Geshe (1102-1176) A great Kadampa Bodhisattva who composed the text *Training the Mind in Seven Points,* a commentary to Geshe Langri Tangpa's *Eight Verses of Training the Mind.* He spread the study and practice of training the mind throughout Tibet. See *Universal Compassion.*

Commitments Promises and pledges taken when engaging in certain spiritual practices.

Concentration A mental factor that makes its primary mind remain on its object single-pointedly. See *Joyful Path of Good Fortune* and *Understanding the Mind*.

Contact A mental factor that functions to perceive its object as pleasant, unpleasant, or neutral. See *Understanding the Mind*.

Contaminated aggregate Any of the aggregates of form, feeling, discrimination, compositional factors, and consciousness of a samsaric being. See also *Aggregate*. See *Heart of Wisdom*.

Dakini Land The Pure Land of Heruka and Vajrayogini. In Sanskrit it is called 'Keajra' and in Tibetan 'Dagpa Khachö'. See *Guide to Dakini Land*.

Deity 'Yidam' in Sanskrit. A Tantric enlightened being.

Delusion A mental factor that arises from inappropriate attention and functions to make the mind unpeaceful and uncontrolled. There are three main delusions: ignorance, desirous attachment, and anger. From these arise all the other delusions, such as jealousy, pride, and deluded doubt. See also *Innate delusions* and *Intellectually-formed delusions*. See *Understanding the Mind*.

Desire realm The environment of hell beings, hungry spirits, animals, human beings, demi-gods, and the gods who enjoy the five objects of desire.

Dharmakirti (circa 6th to 7th century AD) A great Indian Buddhist Yogi and scholar who composed *Commentary to Valid Cognition*, a commentary to *Compendium of Valid Cognition*, which was written by his Spiritual Guide, Dignaga. See *Understanding the Mind*.

Dharma Protector A manifestation of a Buddha or Bodhisattva, whose main function is to eliminate obstacles and gather all necessary conditions for pure Dharma practitioners. Also called the Sanskrit 'Dharmapala'. See *Heart Jewel*.

Direct perceiver A cognizer that apprehends its manifest object. See *Understanding the Mind*.

Discrimination A mental factor that functions to apprehend the uncommon sign of an object. See *Understanding the Mind*.

Dorje Shugdän A Dharma Protector who is an emanation of the Wisdom Buddha Manjushri. His main functions are to avert the inner and outer obstacles that prevent practitioners from gaining spiritual realizations, and to arrange all the necessary conditions for their spiritual development. See *Heart Jewel*.

Dualistic appearance The appearance to mind of an object together with the inherent existence of that object. See *Heart of Wisdom*.

Eighty indicative conceptions Although we have countless gross conceptual minds, they are all included within the eighty gross conceptions. These are called 'indicative conceptions' because they are conclusive reasons indicating the existence of the subtle minds from which they arise. See *Clear Light of Bliss*.

Elements Earth, water, fire, wind, and space. All matter can be said to be composed of a combination of these elements. There are five inner elements (those that are conjoined with the continuum of a person), and five outer elements (those that are not conjoined with the continuum of a person). These elements are not the same as the earth of a field, the water of a river, and so forth. Rather, the elements of earth, water, fire, wind, and space in broad terms are the properties of solidity, liquidity, heat, movement, and space respectively.

Emanation Animate or inanimate form manifested by Buddhas or high Bodhisattvas to benefit others.

Faith A mental factor that functions principally to eliminate non-faith. Faith is a naturally virtuous mind that functions mainly to oppose the perception of faults in its observed object. There are three types of faith: believing faith, admiring faith, and wishing faith. See *Transform Your Life*, *Joyful Path of Good Fortune*, and *Understanding the Mind*.

Feeling A mental factor that functions to experience pleasant, unpleasant, or neutral objects. See *Understanding the Mind*.

Field of Merit Generally, the Three Jewels. Just as external seeds grow in a field of soil, so the virtuous internal seeds produced by virtuous actions grow in dependence upon Buddha Jewel, Dharma Jewel, and Sangha Jewel. Also known as 'Field for Accumulating Merit'.

Four complete purities A Tantric practice is one that possesses the four complete purities: (1) complete purity of place – the environment is seen as the mandala of the Deity; (2) complete purity of body – ordinary appearance of the body is prevented and the practitioner imagines that he or she possesses the body of a Deity; (3) complete purity of enjoyments – sense enjoyments are transformed into offerings to the Deity; and (4) complete purity of deeds – the practitioner regards all his or her actions as the actions of the Deity. See *Great Treasury of Merit* and *Tantric Grounds and Paths*.

Functioning thing A phenomenon that is produced and disintegrates within a moment. Synonymous with impermanent phenomenon, thing, and product. See also *Impermanent phenomenon*.

Generic image The appearing object of a conceptual mind. A generic image, or mental image, of an object is like a reflection of that object. Conceptual minds know their object through the appearance of a generic image of that object, not by seeing the object directly. See *Heart of Wisdom* and *Understanding the Mind*.

Geshe A title given by Kadampa monasteries to accomplished Buddhist scholars. Contracted form of the Tibetan 'ge wai she nyen', literally meaning 'virtuous friend'.

Ghantapa A great Indian Mahasiddha and a lineage Guru in the Highest Yoga Tantra practice of Vajrayogini. See *Guide to Dakini Land*.

God 'Deva' in Sanskrit. A being of the god realm, the highest of the six realms of samsara. There are many different types of god. Some are desire realm gods, while others are form or formless realm gods. See *Joyful Path of Good Fortune*.

Gyalwa Ensäpa (AD 1505-1566) A great Yogi and Mahamudra lineage Guru who attained enlightenment in three years. See *Great Treasury of Merit*.

Heart Sutra One of several *Perfection of Wisdom Sutras* that Buddha taught. Although much shorter than the other *Perfection of Wisdom Sutras*, it contains explicitly or implicitly their entire meaning. Also known as the *Essence of Wisdom Sutra*. For a full commentary, see *Heart of Wisdom*.

Hell realm The lowest of the six realms of samsara. See *Joyful Path of Good Fortune*.

Hevajra A principal Deity of Mother Tantra. See *Great Treasury of Merit*.

Holy being A being who is worthy of devotion.

Hungry spirit A being of the hungry spirit realm, the second lowest of the six realms of samsara. Also known as 'Hungry ghost'. See *Joyful Path of Good Fortune*.

Ignorance A mental factor that is confused about the ultimate nature of phenomena. See *Understanding the Mind*.

Impermanent phenomenon Phenomena are either permanent or impermanent. 'Impermanent' means 'momentary'; thus an impermanent phenomenon is a phenomenon that is produced and disintegrates within a moment. Synonyms of impermanent phenomenon are 'functioning thing', 'thing', and 'product'. There are two types of impermanence: gross and subtle. Gross impermanence is any impermanence that can be seen by an ordinary sense awareness – for example the ageing and death of a sentient being. Subtle impermanence is the momentary disintegration of a functioning thing. See *Heart of Wisdom*.

Imprint There are two types of imprint: imprints of actions and imprints of delusions. Every action we perform leaves an imprint on the mental consciousness, and these imprints are karmic potentialities to experience certain effects in the future. The imprints left by delusions remain even after the delusions themselves have been abandoned, rather as the smell of garlic lingers in a container after the garlic has been removed. Imprints of delusions are obstructions to omniscience, and are completely abandoned only by Buddhas.

Inferential cognizer A completely reliable cognizer whose object is realized in direct dependence upon a conclusive reason. See *Understanding the Mind.*

Innate delusions Delusions that are not the product of intellectual speculation, but that arise naturally. See *Understanding the Mind.*

Inner fire 'Tummo' in Tibetan. An inner heat located at the centre of the navel channel wheel. See *Clear Light of Bliss.*

Intellectually-formed delusions Delusions that arise as a result of relying upon incorrect reasoning or mistaken tenets. See *Understanding the Mind.*

Intention A mental factor that functions to move its primary mind to the object. It functions to engage the mind in virtuous, non-virtuous, and neutral objects. All bodily and verbal actions are initiated by the mental factor intention. See *Understanding the Mind*.

Intermediate state 'Bardo' in Tibetan. The state between death and rebirth. It begins the moment the consciousness leaves the body, and ceases the moment the consciousness enters the body of the next life. See *Joyful Path of Good Fortune* and *Clear Light of Bliss*.

Jealousy A deluded mental factor that feels displeasure when observing others' enjoyments, good qualities, or good fortune. See *Understanding the Mind*.

Je Tsongkhapa (AD 1357-1419) An emanation of the Wisdom Buddha Manjushri, whose appearance in fourteenth-century Tibet as a monk, and the holder of the lineage of pure view and pure deeds, was prophesied by Buddha. He spread a very pure Buddhadharma throughout Tibet, showing how to combine the practices of Sutra and Tantra, and how to practise pure Dharma during degenerate times. His tradition later became known as the 'Gelug', or 'Ganden Tradition'. See *Heart Jewel* and *Great Treasury of Merit*.

Kadam Emanation Scripture Also known as 'Ganden Emanation Scripture'. A special scripture, the nature of Manjushri's wisdom, revealed directly to Je Tsongkhapa by Manjushri. It contains instructions on Vajrayana Mahamudra, *Offering to the Spiritual Guide* (*Lama Chöpa*), *The Hundreds of Deities of the Joyful Land* (*Ganden Lhagyäma*), the *Migtsema* prayer, and six sadhanas of Manjushri. This scripture was not composed in ordinary letters, and only highly realized beings can consult it directly. At first the instructions from this scripture were passed down only by word of mouth from Teacher to disciple, and so the lineage became known as the 'Uncommon Whispered Lineage of the Virtuous Tradition' or the 'Ensa Whispered Lineage'. It is also known as the 'Uncommon Close Lineage' because it was revealed directly to Je

Tsongkhapa by Manjushri. Later, scholars such as the first Panchen Lama (AD 1569-1662) wrote down the instructions from this scripture in ordinary letters. See *Great Treasury of Merit* and *Heart Jewel*.

Kadampa A Tibetan word in which 'Ka' means 'word' and refers to all Buddha's teachings, 'dam' refers to Atisha's special Lamrim instructions known as the 'stages of the path to enlightenment', and 'pa' refers to a follower of Kadampa Buddhism who integrates all the teachings of Buddha that they know into their Lamrim practice. See also *Kadampa Tradition*.

Kadampa Tradition The pure tradition of Buddhism established by Atisha. Followers of this tradition up to the time of Je Tsongkhapa are known as 'Old Kadampas', and those after the time of Je Tsongkhapa are known as 'New Kadampas'. See also *Kadampa* .

Karma Sanskrit word meaning 'action'. Through the force of intention, we perform actions with our body, speech, and mind, and all of these actions produce effects. The effect of virtuous actions is happiness and the effect of negative actions is suffering. See *Joyful Path of Good Fortune*.

Lineage A line of instruction that has been passed down from Spiritual Guide to disciple, with each Spiritual Guide in the line having gained personal experience of the instruction before passing it on to others.

Lineage Gurus The line of Spiritual Guides through whom a particular instruction has been passed down.

Living being Synonymous with sentient being (Tib. sem chän). Any being who possesses a mind that is contaminated by delusions or their imprints. Both 'living being' and 'sentient being' are terms used to distinguish beings whose minds are contaminated by either of these two obstructions from Buddhas, whose minds are completely free from these obstructions.

Lord of Death Although the mara of uncontrolled death is not a sentient being, it is personified as the Lord of Death, or 'Yama'. The Lord of Death is depicted in the diagram of the Wheel of Life clutching the wheel between his claws and teeth. See *Joyful Path of Good Fortune.*

Losang Dragpa The ordained name of Je Tsongkhapa. 'Sumati Kirti' in Sanskrit. See *Great Treasury of Merit.*

Madhyamika A Sanskrit term, literally meaning 'Middle Way'. The higher of the two schools of Mahayana tenets. The Madhyamika view was taught by Buddha in the *Perfection of Wisdom Sutras* during the second turning of the Wheel of Dharma and was subsequently elucidated by Nagarjuna and his followers. There are two divisions of this school, Madhyamika-Svatantrika and Madhyamika-Prasangika, of which the latter is Buddha's final view. See *Meaningful to Behold* and *Ocean of Nectar.*

Mahasiddha Sanskrit term for 'Greatly Accomplished One', which is used to refer to Yogis or Yoginis with high attainments.

Mahayana Sanskrit term for 'Great Vehicle', the spiritual path to great enlightenment. The Mahayana goal is to attain Buddhahood for the benefit of all sentient beings by completely abandoning delusions and their imprints. See *Joyful Path of Good Fortune* and *Meaningful to Behold.*

Maitreya The embodiment of the loving kindness of all Buddhas. At the time of Buddha Shakyamuni, he manifested as a Bodhisattva disciple in order to show Buddha's disciples how to be perfect Mahayana disciples. In the future, he will manifest as the fifth founding Buddha.

Mala A rosary used to count recitations of prayers or mantras, usually with one hundred and eight beads.

Mandala Usually the celestial mansion in which a Tantric Deity abides, or the environment or Deities of a Buddha's Pure Land.

Manjushri The embodiment of the wisdom of all Buddhas. At the time of Buddha Shakyamuni, he manifested as a Bodhisattva disciple in order to show Buddha's disciples how to be perfect Mahayana disciples. See *Great Treasury of Merit* and *Heart Jewel*.

Mantra A Sanskrit word, literally meaning 'mind protection'. Mantra protects the mind from ordinary appearances and conceptions. There are four types of mantra: mantras that are mind, mantras that are inner wind, mantras that are sound, and mantras that are form. In general, there are three types of mantra recitation: verbal recitation, mental recitation, and vajra recitation. See *Tantric Grounds and Paths*.

Mara 'Mara' is Sanskrit for 'demon', and refers to anything that obstructs the attainment of liberation or enlightenment. There are four principal types of mara: the mara of the delusions, the mara of contaminated aggregates, the mara of uncontrolled death, and the Devaputra maras. Of these, only the last are actual sentient beings. See *Heart of Wisdom*.

Meditation Meditation is a mind that concentrates on a virtuous object, and is a mental action that is the main cause of mental peace. There are two types of meditation – analytical meditation and placement meditation. When we use our imagination, mindfulness, and powers of reasoning to find our object of meditation, this is analytical meditation. When we find our object and hold it single-pointedly, this is placement meditation. There are different types of object. Some, such as impermanence or emptiness, are objects apprehended by the mind. Others, such as love, compassion, and renunciation, are actual states of mind. We engage in analytical meditation until the specific object that we seek appears clearly to our mind or until the particular state of mind that we wish to generate arises. This object or state of mind is our object of placement meditation. See *The New Meditation Handbook*.

Mental awareness All minds are included within the five sense awarenesses and mental awareness. There are two types of mental awareness: conceptual mental awareness and non-conceptual mental awareness. Conceptual mental awareness and conceptual mind are synonyms. See *Understanding the Mind*.

Mental continuum The continuum of a mind that has no beginning and no end.

Mental factor A cognizer that principally apprehends a particular attribute of an object. There are fifty-one specific mental factors. Each moment of mind comprises a primary mind and various mental factors. See *Understanding the Mind*.

Mere appearance All phenomena are mere appearance because they are imputed by mind in dependence upon a suitable basis of imputation appearing to mind. The word 'mere' excludes any possibility of inherent existence. See *Ocean of Nectar*.

Merit The good fortune created by virtuous actions. It is the potential power to increase our good qualities and produce happiness.

Migrator A being within samsara who migrates from one uncontrolled rebirth to another.

Migtsema A special prayer of praise and requests to Je Tsongkhapa composed by Manjushri in the *Kadam Emanation Scripture*. The prayer appears in various forms, such as the nine-line and five-line versions. This prayer is very blessed, and those who recite it with faith are able to accomplish great results. See *Heart Jewel*.

Milarepa (1040-1123) A great Tibetan Buddhist meditator and disciple of Marpa, celebrated for his beautiful songs of realization.

Mindfulness A mental factor that functions not to forget the object realized by the primary mind. See *Understanding the Mind* and *Clear Light of Bliss*.

Moral discipline A virtuous mental determination to abandon any fault, or a bodily or verbal action motivated by such a determination. See *Joyful Path of Good Fortune* and *Meaningful to Behold*.

Nada A three-curved line that appears above certain seed-letters.

Nagarjuna A great Indian Buddhist scholar and meditation master who revived the Mahayana in the first century AD by bringing to light the teachings on the *Perfection of Wisdom Sutras*. Nagarjuna's extraordinary life and works were prophesied by Buddha Shakyamuni. See *Ocean of Nectar*.

Naropa (AD 1016-1100) An Indian Buddhist Mahasiddha. See *Guide to Dakini Land*.

Negated object An object explicitly negated by a mind realizing a negative phenomenon. In meditation on emptiness, or lack of inherent existence, it refers to inherent existence. Also known as 'object of negation'.

Object of negation See *Negated object*.

Obstructions to liberation Obstructions that prevent the attainment of liberation. All delusions, such as ignorance, attachment, and anger, together with their seeds, are obstructions to liberation. Also called 'delusion-obstructions'.

Obstructions to omniscience The imprints of delusions, which prevent simultaneous and direct realization of all phenomena. Only Buddhas have overcome these obstructions.

Perfection of Wisdom Sutras Sutras of the second turning of the Wheel of Dharma, in which Buddha revealed his final view of the ultimate nature of all phenomena – emptiness of inherent existence. See *Heart of Wisdom* and *Ocean of Nectar*.

Permanent phenomenon Phenomena are either permanent or impermanent. A permanent phenomenon is a phenomenon that lacks the characteristics of production, abiding, and disintegration.

Person An I imputed in dependence upon any of the five aggregates. Person, being, self, and I are synonyms. See *Understanding the Mind*.

Pratimoksha Sanskrit term for 'personal liberation'. See *The Bodhisattva Vow*.

Primary mind A cognizer that principally apprehends the mere entity of an object. Synonymous with consciousness. There are six primary minds: eye consciousness, ear consciousness, nose consciousness, tongue consciousness, body consciousness, and mental consciousness. Each moment of mind comprises a primary mind and various mental factors. A primary mind and its accompanying mental factors are the same entity but have different functions. See *Understanding the Mind*.

Pure Land A pure environment in which there are no true sufferings. There are many Pure Lands. For example, Tushita is the Pure Land of Buddha Maitreya; Sukhavati is the Pure Land of Buddha Amitabha; and Dakini Land, or Keajra, is the Pure Land of Buddha Vajrayogini and Buddha Heruka. See *Living Meaningfully, Dying Joyfully*.

Purification Generally, any practice that leads to the attainment of a pure body, speech, or mind. More specifically, a practice for purifying negative karma by means of the four opponent powers. See *Joyful Path of Good Fortune*, *The Bodhisattva Vow*, *Universal Compassion*, and *Guide to Dakini Land*.

Realization A stable and non-mistaken experience of a virtuous object that directly protects us from suffering.

Regret A mental factor that feels remorse for actions done in the past. See *Understanding the Mind*.

Sangha According to the Vinaya tradition, any community of four or more fully ordained monks or nuns. In general, ordained or lay people who take Bodhisattva vows or Tantric vows can also be said to be Sangha.

Schools of Buddhist philosophy/tenets Four philosophical views taught by Buddha according to the inclinations and dispositions of disciples. They are the Vaibhashika, Sautrantika, Chittamatra, and Madhyamika schools. The first two are Hinayana schools and the second two are Mahayana schools. They are studied in sequence, the lower tenets being the means by which the higher ones are understood. See *Meaningful to Behold* and *Ocean of Nectar*.

Self-cherishing A mental attitude that considers oneself to be supremely important and precious. It is regarded as a principal object to be abandoned by Bodhisattvas. See *Eight Steps to Happiness* and *Meaningful to Behold*.

Sense awareness All minds are included within sense awareness and mental awareness. There are five types of sense awareness: eye awareness, ear awareness, nose awareness, tongue awareness, and body awareness. See *Understanding the Mind*.

Sense power An inner power located in the very centre of a sense organ that functions directly to produce a sense awareness. There are five sense powers, one for each type of sense awareness – the eye awareness and so forth. They are sometimes known as 'sense powers possessing form'. See *Understanding the Mind*.

Shakyamuni, Buddha The Buddha who is the founder of the Buddhist religion. See *Introduction to Buddhism*.

Shantideva (AD 687-763) A great Indian Buddhist scholar and meditation master. He composed *Guide to the Bodhisattva's Way of Life*. See *Meaningful to Behold*.

Six realms There are six realms of samsara. Listed in ascending order according to the type of karma that causes rebirth in them, they are the realms of the hell beings, hungry spirits, animals, human beings, demi-gods, and gods. The first three are lower realms or unhappy migrations, and the second three are higher realms or happy migrations. See *Joyful Path of Good Fortune*.

Spiritual Guide 'Guru' in Sanskrit, 'Lama' in Tibetan. A Teacher who guides us along the spiritual path. See *Joyful Path of Good Fortune* and *Great Treasury of Merit*.

Superior being 'Arya' in Sanskrit. A being who has a direct realization of emptiness. There are Hinayana Superiors and Mahayana Superiors.

Superior seeing A special wisdom that sees its object clearly, and that is maintained by tranquil abiding and the special suppleness that is induced by investigation. See *Joyful Path of Good Fortune*.

Sutra The teachings of Buddha that are open to everyone to practise without the need for empowerment. These include Buddha's teachings of the three turnings of the Wheel of Dharma.

Three higher trainings Training in moral discipline, concentration, and wisdom motivated by renunciation or bodhichitta.

Torma offering A special food offering made according to either Sutric or Tantric rituals. See *Essence of Vajrayana*.

Tsog offering An offering made by an assembly of Heroes and Heroines. See *Essence of Vajrayana*.

Twelve dependent-related links Dependent-related ignorance, compositional actions, consciousness, name and form, six sources, contact, feeling, craving, grasping, existence, birth, and ageing and death. These twelve links are causes and effects that keep ordinary beings bound within samsara. See *Joyful Path of Good Fortune* and *Heart of Wisdom*.

Vajradhara The founder of Vajrayana, or Tantra. He appears directly only to highly realized Bodhisattvas to whom he gives Tantric teachings. To benefit other living beings with less merit, he manifested the more visible form of Buddha Shakyamuni. He also said that in degenerate times he would appear in an ordinary form as a Spiritual Guide. See *Great Treasury of Merit*.

Vajra Master A fully qualified Tantric Spiritual Guide. See *Great Treasury of Merit*.

Vajrapani The embodiment of the power of all the Buddhas. He appears in a wrathful aspect, displaying his power to overcome outer, inner, and secret obstacles. At the time of Buddha Shakyamuni, he manifested as a Bodhisattva disciple.

Vajrasattva Buddha Vajrasattva is the aggregate of consciousness of all the Buddhas, appearing in the aspect of a white-coloured Deity specifically in order to purify sentient beings' negativity. He is the same nature as Buddha Vajradhara, differing only in aspect. The practice of meditation and recitation of Vajrasattva is a very powerful method for purifying our impure mind and actions. See *Guide to Dakini Land*.

Valid cognizer A cognizer that is non-deceptive with respect to its engaged object. There are two types: inferential valid cognizers and direct valid cognizers. See *Understanding the Mind*.

Vow A virtuous determination to abandon particular faults that is generated in conjunction with a traditional ritual. The three sets of vows are the Pratimoksha vows of individual liberation, the Bodhisattva vows, and the Secret Mantra vows. See *The Bodhisattva Vow* and *Tantric Grounds and Paths*.

Wisdom A virtuous, intelligent mind that makes its primary mind realize its object thoroughly. A wisdom is a spiritual path that functions to release our mind from delusions or their imprints. An example of wisdom is the correct view of emptiness. See *Heart of Wisdom* and *Understanding the Mind*.

Wrong awareness A cognizer that is mistaken with respect to its engaged object. See *Understanding the Mind*.

Yoga A term used for various spiritual practices that entail maintaining a special view, such as Guru yoga and the yogas of sleeping, rising, and experiencing nectar. 'Yoga' also refers to 'union', such as the union of tranquil abiding and superior seeing. See *Guide to Dakini Land*.

Yogi/Yogini Sanskrit words usually referring to a male or a female meditator who has attained the union of tranquil abiding and superior seeing.

Bibliography

Geshe Kelsang Gyatso is a highly respected meditation master and scholar of the Mahayana Buddhist tradition founded by Je Tsongkhapa. Since arriving in the West in 1977, Geshe Kelsang has worked tirelessly to establish pure Buddhadharma throughout the world. Over this period he has given extensive teachings on the major scriptures of the Mahayana. These teachings are currently being published and provide a comprehensive presentation of the essential Sutra and Tantra practices of Mahayana Buddhism.

Books

The following books by Geshe Kelsang are all published by Tharpa Publications.

The Bodhisattva Vow. A practical guide to helping others.
    (2nd. edn., 1995)
Clear Light of Bliss. Tantric meditation manual. (2nd. edn., 1992)
Eight Steps to Happiness. The Buddhist way of loving kindness.
    (2000)

Essence of Vajrayana. The Highest Yoga Tantra practice of Heruka body mandala. (1997)

Great Treasury of Merit. The practice of relying upon a Spiritual Guide. (1992)

Guide to Dakini Land. The Highest Yoga Tantra practice of Buddha Vajrayogini. (2nd. edn., 1996)

Guide to the Bodhisattva's Way of Life. How to enjoy a life of great meaning and altruism. (A translation of Shantideva's famous verse masterpiece.) (2002)

Heart Jewel. The essential practices of Kadampa Buddhism. (2nd. edn., 1997)

Heart of Wisdom. An explanation of the *Heart Sutra.* (4th. edn., 2001)

How to Solve Our Human Problems. The four noble truths. (2005)

Introduction to Buddhism. An explanation of the Buddhist way of life. (2nd. edn., 2001)

Joyful Path of Good Fortune. The complete Buddhist path to enlightenment. (2nd. edn., 1995)

Living Meaningfully, Dying Joyfully. The profound practice of transference of consciousness. (1999)

Mahamudra Tantra. The supreme Heart Jewel nectar. (2005)

Meaningful to Behold. The Bodhisattva's way of life. (4th. edn., 1994)

The New Meditation Handbook. Meditations to make our life happy and meaningful. (2003)

Ocean of Nectar. The true nature of all things. (1995)

Tantric Grounds and Paths. How to enter, progress on, and complete the Vajrayana path. (1994)

Transform Your Life. A blissful journey. (2001)

Understanding the Mind. The nature and power of the mind. (2nd. edn., 1997)

Universal Compassion. Inspiring solutions for difficult times. (4th. edn., 2002)

Sadhanas

Geshe Kelsang has also supervised the translation of a collection of essential sadhanas, or prayer booklets.

Assembly of Good Fortune. The tsog offering for Heruka body mandala.

Avalokiteshvara Sadhana. Prayers and requests to the Buddha of Compassion.

The Bodhisattva's Confession of Moral Downfalls. The purification practice of the *Mahayana Sutra of the Three Superior Heaps.*

Condensed Essence of Vajrayana. Condensed Heruka body mandala self-generation sadhana.

Dakini Yoga. Six-session Guru yoga combined with self-generation as Vajrayogini.

Drop of Essential Nectar. A special fasting and purification practice in conjunction with Eleven-faced Avalokiteshvara.

Essence of Good Fortune. Prayers for the six preparatory practices for meditation on the stages of the path to enlightenment.

Essence of Vajrayana. Heruka body mandala self-generation sadhana according to the system of Mahasiddha Ghantapa.

Feast of Great Bliss. Vajrayogini self-initiation sadhana.

Great Compassionate Mother. The sadhana of Arya Tara.

Great Liberation of the Father. Preliminary prayers for Mahamudra meditation in conjunction with Heruka practice.

Great Liberation of the Mother. Preliminary prayers for Mahamudra meditation in conjunction with Vajrayogini practice.

The Great Mother. A method to overcome hindrances and obstacles by reciting the *Essence of Wisdom Sutra* (the *Heart Sutra*).

Heartfelt Prayers. Funeral service for cremations and burials.

Heart Jewel. The Guru yoga of Je Tsongkhapa combined with the condensed sadhana of his Dharma Protector.

The Kadampa Way of Life. The essential practice of Kadam Lamrim.

Liberation from Sorrow. Praises and requests to the Twenty-one Taras.

Mahayana Refuge Ceremony and Bodhisattva Vow Ceremony.

Medicine Buddha Sadhana. The method for making requests to the Assembly of Seven Medicine Buddhas.

Meditation and Recitation of Solitary Vajrasattva.

Melodious Drum Victorious in all Directions. The extensive fulfilling and restoring ritual of the Dharma Protector, the great king Dorje Shugdän, in conjunction with Mahakala, Kalarupa, Kalindewi, and other Dharma Protectors.

Offering to the Spiritual Guide (Lama Chöpa). A special Guru yoga practice of Je Tsongkhapa's tradition.

Path of Compassion for the Deceased. Powa sadhana for the benefit of the deceased.

Pathway to the Pure Land. Training in powa – the transference of consciousness.

Powa Ceremony. Transference of consciousness for the deceased.

Prayers for Meditation. Brief preparatory prayers for meditation.

A Pure Life. The practice of taking and keeping the eight Mahayana precepts.

The Quick Path. A condensed practice of Heruka Five Deities according to Master Ghantapa's tradition.

Quick Path to Great Bliss. Vajrayogini self-generation sadhana.

Treasury of Blessings. The condensed meaning of Vajrayana Mahamudra and prayers of request to the lineage Gurus.

Treasury of Wisdom. The sadhana of Venerable Manjushri.

Union of No More Learning. Heruka body mandala self-initiation sadhana.

Vajra Hero Yoga. A brief essential practice of Heruka body mandala self-generation, and condensed six-session yoga.

The Vows and Commitments of Kadampa Buddhism.

Wishfulfilling Jewel. The Guru yoga of Je Tsongkhapa combined with the sadhana of his Dharma Protector.

The Yoga of Buddha Vajrapani. The self-generation sadhana of Buddha Vajrapani.

The Yoga of Buddha Amitayus. A special method for increasing lifespan, wisdom, and merit.
The Yoga of White Tara, Buddha of Long Life.

To order any of our publications, or to
receive a catalogue, please contact:

Tharpa Publications
Conishead Priory
Ulverston
Cumbria, LA12 9QQ
England

Tel: 01229-588599
Fax: 01229-483919

E-mail: tharpa@tharpa.com
Website: www.tharpa.com

or

Tharpa Publications
47 Sweeney Road
P.O. Box 430
Glen Spey, NY 12737
USA

Tel: 845-856-5102 or
888-741-3475 (toll free)
Fax: 845-856-2110

Email: sales@tharpa-us.com
Website: www.tharpa.com

- NKT -

Study Programmes of Kadampa Buddhism

Kadampa Buddhism is a Mahayana Buddhist school founded by the great Indian Buddhist Master Atisha (AD 982-1054). His followers are known as 'Kadampas'. 'Ka' means 'word' and refers to Buddha's teachings, and 'dam' refers to Atisha's special Lamrim instructions known as 'the stages of the path to enlightenment'. By integrating their knowledge of all Buddha's teachings into their practice of Lamrim, and by integrating this into their everyday lives, Kadampa Buddhists are encouraged to use Buddha's teachings as practical methods for transforming daily activities into the path to enlightenment. The great Kadampa Teachers are famous not only for being great scholars, but also for being spiritual practitioners of immense purity and sincerity.

The lineage of these teachings, both their oral transmission and blessings, was then passed from Teacher to disciple, spreading throughout much of Asia, and now to many countries throughout the Western world. Buddha's teachings, which are known as 'Dharma', are likened to a wheel that moves from country to country in accordance with changing conditions and people's karmic inclinations. The external forms of presenting Buddhism may change as it meets with different cultures and societies, but its essential authenticity is ensured through the continuation of an unbroken lineage of realized practitioners.

Kadampa Buddhism was first introduced into the West in 1977 by the renowned Buddhist Master, Venerable Geshe Kelsang Gyatso. Since that time, he has worked tirelessly to spread Kadampa Buddhism throughout the world by giving extensive teachings, writing many profound texts on Kadampa Buddhism, and founding the New Kadampa Tradition – International Kadampa Buddhist Union (NKT–IKBU), which now has over eight hundred Kadampa Buddhist Centres worldwide. Each Centre offers study programmes on Buddhist psychology, philosophy, and meditation instruction, as well as retreats for all levels of practitioner. The emphasis is on integrating Buddha's teachings into daily life to solve our human problems and to spread lasting peace and happiness throughout the world.

The Kadampa Buddhism of the NKT–IKBU is an entirely independent Buddhist tradition and has no political affiliations. It is an association of Buddhist Centres and practitioners that derive their inspiration and guidance from the example of the ancient Kadampa Buddhist Masters and their teachings, as presented by Geshe Kelsang.

There are three reasons why we need to study and practise the teachings of Buddha: to develop our wisdom, to cultivate a good heart, and to maintain a peaceful state of mind. If we do not strive to develop our wisdom, we will always remain ignorant of ultimate truth – the true nature of reality. Although we wish for happiness, our ignorance leads us to engage in non-virtuous actions, which are the main cause of all our suffering. If we do not cultivate a good heart, our selfish motivation destroys harmony and good relationships with others. We have no peace, and no chance to gain pure happiness. Without inner peace, outer peace is impossible. If we do not maintain a peaceful state of mind, we are not happy even if we have ideal conditions. On the other hand, when our mind is peaceful, we are happy, even if our external conditions are unpleasant. Therefore, the development of these qualities is of utmost importance for our daily happiness.

Geshe Kelsang Gyatso, or 'Geshe-la' as he is affectionately called by his students, has designed three special spiritual programmes for the systematic study and practice of Kadampa Buddhism that are especially suited to the modern world – the General Programme (GP), the Foundation Programme (FP), and the Teacher Training Programme (TTP).

GENERAL PROGRAMME

The General Programme provides a basic introduction to Buddhist view, meditation, and practice that is suitable for beginners. It also includes advanced teachings and practice from both Sutra and Tantra.

FOUNDATION PROGRAMME

The Foundation Programme provides an opportunity to deepen our understanding and experience of Buddhism through a systematic study of five texts:

1 *Joyful Path of Good Fortune* – a commentary to Atisha's Lamrim instructions, the stages of the path to enlightenment.
2 *Universal Compassion* – a commentary to Bodhisattva Chekhawa's *Training the Mind in Seven Points*.
3 *Heart of Wisdom* – a commentary to the *Heart Sutra*.
4 *Meaningful to Behold* – a commentary to Bodhisattva Shantideva's *Guide to the Bodhisattva's Way of Life*.
5 *Understanding the Mind* – a detailed explanation of the mind, based on the works of the Buddhist scholars Dharmakirti and Dignaga.

The benefits of studying and practising these texts are as follows:

(1) *Joyful Path of Good Fortune* – we gain the ability to put all Buddha's teachings of both Sutra and Tantra into practice. We can easily make progress on, and complete, the stages of the path to the supreme happiness of enlightenment. From a practical point of view, Lamrim is the main body of Buddha's teachings, and the other teachings are like its limbs.

(2) *Universal Compassion* – we gain the ability to integrate Buddha's teachings into our daily life and solve all our human problems.

(3) *Heart of Wisdom* – we gain a realization of the ultimate nature of reality. By gaining this realization, we can eliminate the ignorance of self-grasping, which is the root of all our suffering.

(4) *Meaningful to Behold* – we transform our daily activities into the Bodhisattva's way of life, thereby making every moment of our human life meaningful.

(5) *Understanding the Mind* – we understand the relationship between our mind and its external objects. If we understand that objects depend upon the subjective mind, we can change the way objects appear to us by changing our own mind. Gradually, we will gain the ability to control our mind and in this way solve all our problems.

TEACHER TRAINING PROGRAMME

The Teacher Training Programme is designed for people who wish to train as authentic Dharma Teachers. In addition to completing the study of twelve texts of Sutra and Tantra, which include the five texts mentioned above, the student is required to observe certain commitments with regard to behaviour and way of life, and to complete a number of meditation retreats.

All Kadampa Buddhist Centres are open to the public. Every year we celebrate Festivals in many countries throughout the world, including two in England, where people gather from around the world to receive special teachings and empowerments and to enjoy a spiritual holiday. Please feel free to visit us at any time!

For further information, please contact:

UK NKT Office
Manjushri Kadampa Meditation Centre
Conishead Priory
Ulverston
Cumbria, LA12 9QQ
England

Tel/Fax: 01229-588533

Email: kadampa@dircon.co.uk
Website: www.kadampa.org

or

US NKT Office
Kadampa Meditation Center
47 Sweeney Road
P.O. Box 447
Glen Spey, NY 12737
USA

Tel: 845-856-9000
Fax: 845-856-2110

Email: info@kadampacenter.org
Website: www.kadampacenter.org

Index

The letter 'g' indicates an entry in the glossary.

C

O

P